STRESS 101

An overview for Teens

STRESS 101

An overview for Teens

Margaret O. Hyde

Elizabeth H. Forsyth, M.D.

Twenty-First Century Books
Minneapolis

Text copyright © 2008 by Margaret O. Hyde and Elizabeth H. Forsyth

Twenty-First Century Books
A division of Lerner Publishing Group, Inc.
241 First Avenue North
Minneapolis, Minnesota 55401 U.S.A.

Website address: www.lernerbooks.com

Library of Congress Cataloging in Publication Data

Hyde, Margaret O. (Margaret Oldroyd)
    Stress 101 : an overview for teens / by Margaret O. Hyde and Elizabeth H.
Forsyth.
        p.   cm. – (Teen overviews)
    Includes bibliographical references and index.
    ISBN 978–0–8225–6788–2 (lib. bdg. : alk. paper)
    1. Stress management for teenagers. 2. Stress in adolescence. 3. Stress
(Psychology) I. Forsyth, Elizabeth Held. II. Title. III. Title: Stress one hundred
and one. IV. Title: Stress one hundred one.
RA785.H93 2008
616.9'800835—dc22   2007027631

Manufactured in the United States of America
1 2 3 4 5 6 – BP – 13 12 11 10 09 08

Contents

Chapter 1

What Does Stress Mean to You?

Tests! Peer Pressure! House rules! Sports tryouts! Roller coaster rides! Clothes! Alcohol! Smoking! Terrorists! Bullies! Illnesses! Injuries! And more!

Stress is with you every day. Some stress is good, and some stress is bad. How can you enjoy more good stress? What can you do about the bad stress? And what exactly is stress anyway?

If you ask someone if he or she knows what stress is, the answer will probably be yes. Then ask the person to define stress. That is not so easy. A report from the Harvard Medical School defines stress as any real or imagined danger or situation that requires adjustment to change. The danger may be a challenge or a threat. Or it can be any kind of change that requires you to adapt. Stress is anything in the environment that causes you to react.

Anything that causes change in your life causes stress. Dr. Hans Selye, who is considered the father of stress research, noted that the body has a similar set of responses to many different kinds of trauma or demands. Physical and psychological stresses trigger the same kinds of responses. If you break your leg, your body suffers stress. An injury of any sort will stress the body. But most people think of psychological pressures (stress of the mind) or emotional upset (stress of feelings) when they talk about stress. This book focuses on those types of stress.

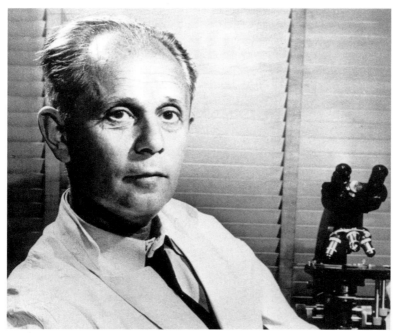

Dr. Hans Selye worked for many years at the University of Montreal in Montreal, Quebec, Canada. He wrote more than thirty books dealing with stress.

If You Are Alive, You Have Stress

Big or small, serious or incidental, good or bad—stress is a part of being human. If you are alive, you have stress. From taking a quiz to college boards, from a minor inconvenience to a major life event, some stress occurs in everyone's life. To Shana, stress is the arguing and disruption accompanying her parents' impending divorce. Where will she live? Will she have to change schools? Will she lose all her friends? To Liam, stress is trying to pass chemistry. He gets an A in all his other classes, but he hates chemistry because it is so hard for him. He feels stress as he walks toward the lab. Some days seem more stressful than others, but there is always some amount of stress to deal with.

Stress means different things to different people. Stress can be a large Irish setter walking down the street by itself. Seventeen-year-old Ashley is afraid of dogs. Her friend Caleb, who is walking with her, loves dogs, but Ashley has been afraid of them ever since she was bitten by a large dog several years ago. Someone has told her that dogs can sense fear and they are more apt to attack people who are afraid of them, so this makes her fear worse.

Some stresses are good for you, and some are bad. Good stress can make you excel in speeches, exams, and sports. Suppose you've worked hard preparing a speech for tomorrow, but you still feel nervous about public speaking. You keep telling yourself you have to talk for only twenty minutes, but just thinking about standing in front of everyone in the school makes you feel weak. The stress you feel influences you to do a thorough job preparing the speech, and that is good

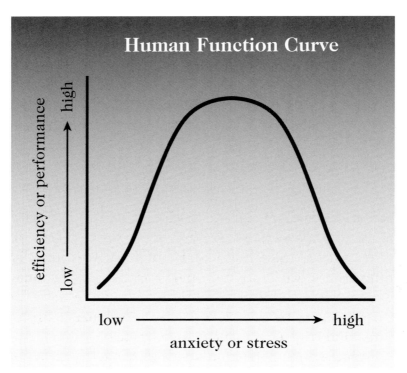

Human Function Curve

efficiency or performance — low → high

anxiety or stress — low → high

A small amount of stress can be good for you, while too much stress can be harmful. The first part of the curve (upward) shows how performance improves with a small amount of stress. The second part of the curve (downward) shows the reduced capacity and impaired health from excessive stress.

stress. When stress interferes with your sleep and memory, it is harmful. But then stress may decrease when you start to give the speech. You realize that you aren't going to freeze and forget what you wanted to say.

Good stress for one person can be bad stress for someone else. To Megan, stress is the wonderful birthday she will celebrate with her friends at the movies.

She can ask only ten of them, and it is stressful deciding which friends to ask. But the stress of the party will be good stress. The movie, which promises to jolt you out of your seat, will bring a different kind of good stress. Some people pay money to experience this kind of stress in movies; on roller coasters; and while parachute jumping, hang gliding, or white-water rafting.

Acute Stress

You experience many small stresses day to day, and most of them are short-lived. A certain degree of stress is necessary for living, and the body usually returns to normal after a time of fear or excitement. Even extremely stressful events, such as the death of a family member or close friend, are usually finite. This kind of stress is called acute stress.

Acute stress is the kind of stress that sets your body in a fight-or-flight mode for a short time. Suppose a masked man points a gun at you and demands your money. Your body responds to the stress, ready to fight or run (take flight). Your heart is racing; you are breathing hard; your blood pressure is up; you are perspiring; your sight, hearing, and other senses are heightened; and special chemicals rage around your body.

You know you dare not do anything other than what the mugger tells you to do. You give the mugger your wallet, and he takes off with it. You quickly pull your cell phone from your pocket and dial 911. When help comes, the support of other people allows you to deal with your stress. Before long, your body returns to normal.

A classic example of acute stress is when a zebra encounters a lion in the wild. What happens in the zebra's body is somewhat like your reaction to a masked man. The lion charges out of the bushes, attacks the zebra, and splits open the skin on its abdomen, but the zebra gets away. The lion and the zebra are under stress during the attack. The zebra's fight-or-flight responses are in full force as it struggles to get away from the lion. Both animals experience a highly stressful situation for a short time, but when the attack is over, their stress responses return to normal.

Even though the stressful experience brings about a large number of changes in the bodies of these animals, the changes do not last long. The lion does not plan or get excited about another stressful attack on a zebra, nor does the lion become stressed by remembering the attack. And although zebras instinctively try to avoid lions, the injured zebra does not worry about meeting a lion tomorrow or next week. Zebras and lions don't suffer from psychological stress.

Adrenaline Junkies

Some people thrive on the excitement of acute stress. To them, stress provides wonderful adventure and they are willing to take serious risks to get excitement. Stress seekers include politicians, mountain climbers, white-water rafters, stunt pilots, bungee jumpers, race car drivers, and many others who enjoy exciting activities. They are sometimes called adrenaline junkies because they seek activities that increase the flow of the hormone adrenaline.

Michael was always a risk taker, so when a friend of his father asked if he would like to learn to parachute jump, he was ready immediately. First, he had some sessions of instruction. After that he was assigned to an instructor. Michael was very excited to do a tandem jump. His instructor fastened a harness to Michael in four places while they were in the airplane. In a sense, the instructor "wore" Michael on the front, and his main and reserve canopies were on his back. After the first landing, Michael was hooked. He even took an extra job to earn money for this expensive hobby.

Each time Michael reached the airport, he began to experience a little anxiety. As he boarded the airplane, he became more and more apprehensive. Each time his parachute was strapped to his back, the instructor reviewed exactly what would happen—even if Michael became too frightened to pull the cord—but the stress was still there. As they flew to the spot where the jump would take place, Michael's response to the stress always reached a new high. But then when he stepped outside the plane, he lost some of his anxiety. The decision about whether to jump had been made. When he sailed toward the ground, he was conscious of the joy but none of the fear. His worries were over, and he tumbled safely onto the ground. Michael sought this kind of stress again and again.

Extreme Acute Stress

In rare cases, acute stress can be so severe in humans that it can cause death. An unusual but dramatic example of extreme, acute stress is seen in the voodoo death. Voodoo death is when someone dies from the effects of voodoo, a set of religious beliefs. This can happen in dozens of ways. Sorcerers might use carved wooden dolls, different kinds of bones, or just an evil eye to bring on stress that can be lethal.

For example, an Aborigine sorcerer in Australia carries some bones from a giant lizard. He points them at a thief who has stolen his brother's food. Since childhood, this thief has been taught to fear the sorcerer's bones and to expect disaster. He reacts strongly when the bones are pointed at him. He holds up his hands as if they could stop the deadly forces he believes are pouring into his body. He hears the death knell, and he knows it is for him. He tries to shriek, but he can't. His face becomes distorted, and his whole body trembles. He falls to the ground.

After a while, he seems to grow calm and he returns to the shelter where he lives. He stays there, having nothing to do with his family or other members of his tribe. He grows sicker day by day as he refuses to eat. At first, his family brings him food and water, but since he does not eat what they bring, they stop providing for him. He expects death, and it comes to him. The stress of the pointed bones begins acute changes that lead to his starvation and death.

More common cases involve the sudden death of soldiers who had not suffered any wounds. Many of these deaths were reported from the bloody battle-fields of World War I (1914–1918). Some physicians believe these men may have died of shock. Fear, a response to stress, may have produced a surge of stress hormones, resulting in decreased blood flow to their hearts or changes to their normal heart rhythms that led to their death.

In Israel, during the Persian Gulf War (1991), fewer deaths from missiles occurred than from sudden cardiac arrest among frightened, elderly people. Some of these people may have had heart disease, but many of them likely showed no signs of heart trouble.

Stress is probably involved in many deaths that follow personal danger, threat of injury, sudden deaths of loved ones, anniversaries of those deaths, and extreme joy. If a person dies during sex or after winning a prize trip to China, stress has probably set the stage, although in many cases the person might already have had a diseased heart. If the heart is diseased, clogged blood vessels might narrow further and heart rhythm could go out of sync in such a way that the person dies.

But death can occur even without heart disease. Robert Sapolsky, noted author and scientist, cites a case in Vermont where a woman found her husband lying near his tractor. She realized that he had died of heart disease, and she suddenly met her own death. She apparently died from sudden stress. Her autopsy showed no sign of prior heart disease.

Chronic Stress

In many other cases, stress lasts a long time. The body kicks into high gear and stays there. This is called chronic stress. Everyone experiences or has experienced some kind of chronic stress. People who ride the subway to and from work experience many stresses: the noise, the crowds of people, and the delay of a train that stops for no apparent reason in between stations. One man in the crowded subway smells of tobacco, garlic, and body odor, but there is no space to get away from him.

Oliver has a driver who takes him to work. He avoids the stress of the subway ride, but the driver is not always on time. Sometimes he takes roads that are so full of traffic that a long time is spent stopping and starting. Couldn't he have found a better way to go? Oliver has an early meeting. Day after day, he gets uptight about the driver and the traffic.

Emily has a teacher who is very demanding. Emily writes well, but the teacher makes so much fuss about commas and grammar. Emily feels her teacher doesn't appreciate what she writes. Day after day, Emily suffers from the stress of a teacher whose priorities are different from hers.

Humans suffer from chronic stress in many ways. Suppose you are under stress because you are dieting. You have extra demands at school with a term paper due in a few days and finals beginning right after the paper. Before you finish the term paper, you hear reports about a burglar in your neighborhood. You become overloaded with stress. You may develop a habit of worrying about what is going to happen. You keep your body stressed for a long period of time. You have trouble sleeping, and you wake up wired. Stress is affecting your health.

While short-term stress can make you ready to rise to a challenge, the stress response can cause problems if it overreacts or fails to turn off and calm down. Chronic stress can lead to numerous physical symptoms, such as stomach problems, headache, chest pain, or allergic reactions. An overstressed person may develop psychological conditions such as anxiety, depression, panic attacks, or sleeping problems. These conditions can lead to overeating, smoking cigarettes, drinking alcohol, or taking drugs.

Chapter 2

What Stress Does to Your Body

Fifteen-year-old Maia was sitting by the side of the family pool watching her uncle swim laps. Suddenly, he stopped swimming and began to flounder about, barely able to keep his head above water. He looked as if he might be in danger of drowning. Clearly, he needed help immediately.

Without thinking, her heart pounding and her muscles tensing, Maia jumped into the pool and pulled him out. She saved her uncle's life. But how did Maia muster the strength to drag a 150-pound man out of the pool? When Maia recognized the emergency, a message flashed to a structure in her brain called the hypothalamus, triggering a set of complex reactions in her body.

How Your Body Acts

Your brain tells your body what to do by sending signals through nerves. These nerves go from the brain into the spinal cord and from the spinal cord to all parts of your body. The voluntary nervous system is under your conscious control. For instance, if you want to pick up a pencil, your brain sends messages through the voluntary nerves supplying the muscles of your arm and hand to carry out the appropriate movements.

Another part of the nervous system is the autonomic nervous system. This network governs all the tasks that you don't have to think about and that your body does automatically—such as heartbeat, blood pressure, breathing, and digestion. The autonomic nervous system has two components—the sympathetic and the parasympathetic.

When danger threatens, the sympathetic nervous system revs up and prepares your body for action. It is responsible for the fight-or-flight response. Your heart rate increases, more blood is pumped to your muscles, your pupils dilate, and digestion is slowed.

The parasympathetic nervous system has the opposite effect. It calms your body after the danger has passed. It has been called the rest-and-digest system.

Ready for Action

In the early part of the twentieth century, a Harvard University physiologist named Walter Cannon experimented with cats that were frightened by dogs. He isolated a substance from their adrenal glands (glands that sit on top of the kidneys) and injected it into other cats that were calm. He found that their heart rate and blood pressure increased. The substance he injected was the hormone adrenaline, also known as epinephrine.

The adrenal glands are among a number of special organs in the body known as endocrine glands, which manufacture complex chemicals called hormones. These hormones are released into the bloodstream and act on other organs or parts of the body in various ways. When danger threatens, the hormone adrenaline is the first responder in the process of preparing your body for action. Here's what happens.

The hypothalamus is wired to the autonomic nervous system. In an emergency such as Maia's, the hypothalamus sends a message that is rapidly transmitted through the sympathetic nerves directly to the adrenals. The adrenals immediately begin to pour the stress hormone adrenaline into the bloodstream to start the flight-or-fight response.

The adrenals also secrete other hormones that help the body respond to a threat. These include noradrenaline (norepinephrine) and cortisol. The hypothalamus sends a chemical known as corticotropin-releasing hormone (CRH) to the pituitary, a gland underneath the area of the hypothalamus. CRH stimulates the pituitary to release adrenocorticotropic hormone (ACTH). ACTH travels through the bloodstream to the adrenal glands, stimulating them to release the hormone cortisol.

The hypothalamus, the pituitary, and the adrenal glands make up a system that is known as the hypothalamic-pituitary-adrenal (HPA) axis, or the stress circuit. It controls the activity of many hormones in the body. It also acts to dampen the response if stress hormone levels get too high.

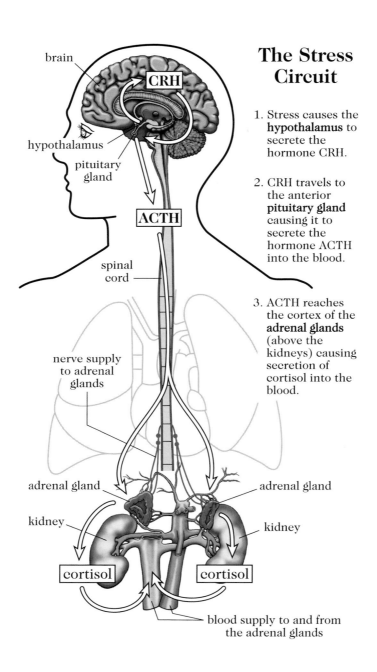

The Stress Circuit

1. Stress causes the **hypothalamus** to secrete the hormone CRH.

2. CRH travels to the anterior **pituitary gland** causing it to secrete the hormone ACTH into the blood.

3. ACTH reaches the cortex of the **adrenal glands** (above the kidneys) causing secretion of cortisol into the blood.

brain

hypothalamus

pituitary gland

spinal cord

nerve supply to adrenal glands

adrenal gland

kidney

adrenal gland

kidney

CRH

ACTH

cortisol

cortisol

blood supply to and from the adrenal glands

Superhuman Acts

The stress circuit is a complicated system that allows you to respond to challenges, influencing systems throughout your body. In an emergency, it's important to get energy to the parts of the body that need it the most and to shut down functions that are not immediately needed. Digestion, repair and growth of body tissues, and sexual arousal are not so important during a crisis, so these systems are suppressed.

Heart rate and blood pressure increase, allowing more blood flow to your large muscles. You breathe more rapidly to provide your body with more oxygen. Blood vessels in your skin narrow so that less blood goes to the skin and less bleeding will occur if you are injured. Your blood clots more easily to decrease the chances of bleeding to death. There's also a reason why your hair stands on end when you are frightened. Sympathetic nerve branches go to very tiny muscles attached to the hairs. When stress activates your sympathetic nervous system, the muscles contract, making the hair stand up.

Stored nutrients are broken down into simpler forms to make them more easily available for energy. Carbohydrates are converted to glucose (sugar), and stored fats are converted to fatty acids and other compounds and released into the bloodstream. The immune system gets ready to fight possible infections. Sight and hearing become keener. Your brain even produces its own natural painkillers called endorphins.

These reactions took place in Maia's body and gave her the extra energy and strength to pull her uncle out of the swimming pool. There are many such accounts of people who performed almost superhuman acts when faced with danger. An old woman lifted up her car to release her cat trapped underneath. In Utah a hiker saved his own life by cutting off his arm with a knife after a huge boulder fell on the arm and trapped him with no possibility of escaping.

During the terrorist attack on the World Trade Center in New York City and on the Pentagon near

Hiker Aron Ralston (center) *cut off his own arm after it became trapped under a boulder while he was climbing in Utah. The severe stress of the incident caused a lifesaving response that would not have been possible under ordinary circumstances. Here he appears with his parents at the hospital where he was treated.*

Washington, D.C., on September 11, 2001, many victims were carried out of the burning buildings. Ordinary citizens and firefighters were able to call up extraordinary reserves of strength to perform heroic feats.

Facing a Challenge

Your body is constantly reacting to the activities in your life. Consider what happens when you wake up in the morning. You go from sleep to consciousness and from lying down to getting out of bed and standing up. To supply the extra energy you need, the level of stress hormones is higher in the morning. Allostasis helps your body meet changing demands.

Allostasis is a word derived from the Greek that means "stability through change." Allostatic systems keep your body stable because they have the ability to change when you are faced with a challenge. This is what happens when the brain, the stress circuit, and the autonomic nervous system all work together to mobilize the rest of the body in response to stress.

The fight-or-flight response is an extreme example of this. Imagine you meet a grizzly bear in the woods. When the bear wanders off and the threat is gone, the feedback mechanism kicks in, as long as your systems are functioning properly. This causes the level of stress hormones to drop and dampens the sympathetic nervous system. The parasympathetic nervous system takes over, and you begin to feel better. Your heart is no longer pounding, your blood pressure drops to its normal level, your breathing slows, and you relax.

But sometimes the system doesn't work properly, and that may cause damage in both animals and people. Dr. Bruce McEwen and other researchers refer to this condition as allostatic load. The mechanism that is designed to adapt and protect the body becomes overwhelmed under certain circumstances. The stress response varies from one person to another, and it is partly influenced by heredity. It can also be affected by extreme stress during any time of life, from before birth through adulthood.

Stress Begins in the Brain

Repeated or chronic stress that activates a person's stress response over and over again can cause disease, especially when the stress is psychological. In general, only in human beings does the stress response remain high, because of the way our thoughts and emotions are connected to the systems that control them. As McEwen has commented, stress begins in the brain.

During an encounter with a lion, a zebra's stress response is activated, but it quickly subsides when the crisis is over. Animals always remain vigilant and on the lookout for predators, but unlike humans, they don't have the mental capacity to worry about when the next lion is going to attack. But under some conditions, even animals can be affected by severe stress. Here is an example.

In the 1930s, the scientist Hans Selye carried out an experiment to find out what would happen if he gave ovarian extract to rats. The extract was a solution made from ovaries, the female reproductive organs, which contain eggs and produce female hormones. A colleague was working with this material, and it interested Selye. He injected one group of rats every day with the extract. When he examined them after several months, he found that they had developed enlarged adrenal glands, shrunken immune system tissues, and stomach ulcers. A stomach ulcer is an inflamed area in the lining of the stomach.

Then he performed the same experiment with another group of rats, the control group. Control groups are used to make certain that the outcome of the experiment is actually the direct result of the procedure or substance being tested. Selye treated the control group exactly the same way as the first group, except that he injected them every day with an inactive salt solution instead of ovarian extract. To his surprise, he found that these rats had developed the same abnormalities as the other rats. Clearly, the results were not caused by the ovarian extract.

Selye was rather clumsy in his attempts at handling the rats. When he tried to inject them, he often dropped them and had to chase them. He concluded that it was the trauma of being mishandled every day for months that had caused the damage to their organs. Repeated stress in human beings can cause similar kinds of damage.

The Stress Response Varies

Some individuals seem to be highly sensitive to situations that don't make others feel stressed. Their response is more extreme than the response most people would have in a similar situation. Their bodies are therefore more frequently flooded with an outpouring of stress hormones. This results in high blood pressure and signs of wear and tear on other systems as well. In some people, the stress response doesn't turn off quickly enough after the stress is over, so their bodies are subjected to stress hormones for long periods of time.

In contrast to situations such as the ones described, in which there is too much stress hormone activity, some people don't produce enough of a stress response. This, too, can have consequences. For example, allergies, asthma, and rheumatoid arthritis are among the conditions that can result from underproduction of the hormone cortisol.

The stress response is a protective mechanism, but when something goes wrong, it can result in serious damage to almost every system of the body. Some of these effects are discussed in the following chapters.

Chapter 3

Stress and the Young Brain

Extreme stress at any time in your life can permanently change the way your body reacts to stressful situations thereafter. Stress can affect you even before you are born. Studies involving rodents and non-human primates have shown that females stressed during pregnancy have offspring that show disturbances in development and behavior. In contrast to rats whose mothers were not stressed during pregnancy, baby rats born of stressed mothers were more timid about exploring and were less able to adapt to new situations. They learned more slowly, and their behavior was not normal. These studies suggest that stress hormones in the mother's blood can enter the circulation of the fetus and influence the development of its nervous system.

Some important brain structures in these animals were also found to be abnormal. The hippocampus is a part of the brain that is involved in the development of memory. Researchers discovered that the hippocampus in these rats was smaller and had fewer synapses (connections between nerve cells) than in normal rats. This finding explains why the animals had learning deficits. In addition, the rats showed changes in the amygdala, the brain region involved in

Some Parts of the Brain Involving the Stress Response

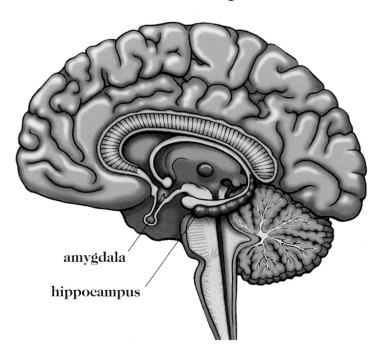

Researchers have discovered that certain parts of the brain, such as the amygdala and the hippocampus, can be damaged by too much stress.

anxiety and fear. This finding may be the reason for the fearful behavior seen in the rats.

It isn't possible to perform controlled experiments with human mothers, so it is much more difficult to judge the effects of prenatal stress in humans than in animals. But many studies have suggested that the effects of stress are similar in human beings. Although the evidence is not as clear-cut, researchers believe that the same mechanisms are at work and that high levels of maternal stress hormones have a damaging effect on the developing fetus.

Six-month-olds born to mothers who were depressed or abused during their pregnancy responded to minor stress with higher-than-normal levels of stress hormones. Some studies have suggested that children exposed to stress before birth are slower to develop and have more behavioral disturbances. Other studies have linked prenatal stress with a higher rate of psychiatric disorders such as schizophrenia and depression in adulthood. One group of eighteen-year-old students in China had mothers who were exposed to the stress of a severe earthquake during pregnancy. These students were found to have a higher incidence of depression compared to a group of students whose mothers had not experienced that stress.

The First Few Years

For a long time, scientists have known that the way babies are treated in the first few years of life is critical in determining the ways their brains develop. Many factors in the environment, both positive and negative, can have an effect on a young child's brain.

29

If an individual is subjected to major stresses in early childhood, he or she may end up with an exaggerated stress response. The person might overreact to relatively minor situations and pump out higher levels of stress hormones with each experience.

Experiments with animals have shown that events during early life can determine the ability to handle stress in later life. In one such experiment, one group of infant rats was removed from their mothers for fifteen minutes a day and then returned. The mothers greeted them with intensive licking and grooming. Another group of infant rats was taken away from their mothers for a period of three hours a day—a highly stressful experience.

When these pups were returned to their mothers, the mothers initially tended to ignore them. These "neglected" baby rats showed excessive levels of stress hormones in later tests, and these effects lasted into adulthood. In contrast, the pups whose mothers groomed and licked them immediately on their return showed normal stress responses.

Researchers studied some infant monkeys raised by mothers who were distressed. The mothers had endured unpredictable food supplies and showed inconsistent and neglectful behavior toward their offspring. Researchers found that the babies had abnormally high levels of stress. They were less social, and they also became abnormally fearful in new situations or during separation from their mothers.

Animals are not the only creatures that need nurturing and protection from stress in their surroundings. When your grandmother was a baby, scientists did not realize that some of the child-rearing practices of the time created an environment that was stressful and potentially damaging to babies. Experts told parents that they shouldn't pick up their infants to comfort them whenever they cried. Experts thought that too much handling was bad and that mothers should feed babies according to a strict schedule. These experts believed that babies needed only to have their physical needs cared for. They thought cuddling and lots of physical contact might be harmful to the child's development.

Doctors kept premature babies isolated in their incubators and discouraged mothers from visiting hospitalized children. It was considered important to control infection by limiting contacts. Many children who lived in orphanages or other institutions where they received little or no mothering appeared listless, apathetic, and depressed; didn't gain weight; and didn't develop normally. A large number of these babies died.

Stress and Child Development

In the 1950s, psychologist Harry Harlow carried out a series of famous experiments with rhesus monkeys that permanently changed child-rearing practices. He removed infant rhesus monkeys from their mothers and placed them in cages with two types of surrogate mothers. Both had wooden heads that resembled monkey heads. One mother had a body constructed of wire mesh, with a milk bottle sticking out of it. The other fake mother had no milk bottle, and her body was wrapped with soft cloth.

Harlow found that the baby monkeys preferred the cloth mothers to the wire mothers, even though the wire mothers had milk. The monkeys nursed from the wire mother's bottle but spent most of their time with the cloth mother. They needed cuddling more than they needed milk. Other scientists criticized Harlow for some of his experiments because they were very cruel and unethical. For example, he kept monkeys in complete isolation, in what he called the pit of despair, to see how they developed. Their behavior became extremely disturbed and abnormal.

But his studies showed that separating infant monkeys from their mothers causes extreme stress and lasting ill effects such as depression and inability to socialize normally with other monkeys. In addition, the animals that were raised with surrogate mothers were unable to mate normally. Those who did mate and had babies didn't know how to care for them and often abused them.

These studies revolutionized the thinking about how children develop emotionally. Harlow showed how important it is for human as well as monkey babies to have affection and early social experiences for them to develop normally. Other researchers agreed. The experts had finally begun to realize that infants do not develop normally if they don't receive enough stimulation and if they lack consistent interaction with a regular caretaker. Cuddling, comforting a crying baby, talking, singing, and providing interesting surroundings are all ways that parents can create a stimulating environment.

People usually recall unpleasant situations when they think about what causes stress—events such as witnessing a shooting or speaking in front of a large audience. But many times, stress can involve a failure to provide something that is needed. In 1986 doctors studied some premature infants who had to be kept isolated in incubators free of germs. Their mothers could not nurse or cuddle them because they were too ill or fragile. Some scientists who were studying newborns noticed that the premature babies were rarely touched, so they began touching

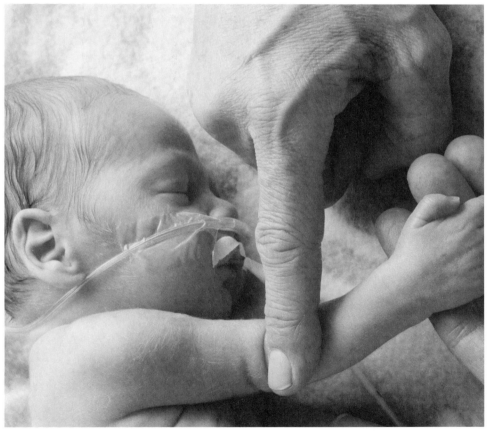

In the 1950s, researchers discovered the benefits of touching and cuddling babies. This adult is giving a gentle massage to a premature baby to help the baby grow stronger.

and stroking them several times a day. Those who were touched grew faster, were more alert, and did better than the premature babies who did not receive this extra attention. Touch is crucial for a baby's development.

Stress Dwarfism

Scientists discovered a condition known as psychosocial short stature (PSS), or stress dwarfism, in orphanages where they saw infants who failed to thrive and grow even though they had enough to eat. They found that continued activation of stress hormones inhibits the release of other hormones that are needed for growth. When the children were placed in environments where they received enough attention, they began to grow normally. The following story is a dramatic example of how emotional stress can affect your body.

A young boy with stress dwarfism was admitted to the hospital. When he arrived at the hospital, the growth hormone level in his blood was very low. While there he became very attached to a nurse who spent a lot of time with him. Three months later, his growth hormone level had more than doubled and he had begun to grow rapidly.

Then the nurse took a three-week vacation. During that period, the boy's growth spurt and levels of growth hormone dropped dramatically, even though he was still eating the same amount of food and nothing had changed except the absence of the nurse. After the nurse returned, his growth hormone level shot back up and he again began growing normally.

Stress and Memory

As noted earlier, some kinds of physical and mental stress are good. Mild or moderate short-term stresses or challenges can help you perform better. Suppose you have an important exam and you're feeling a bit anxious. The stress hormones and the sympathetic nervous system that got turned on are actually helping your memory because they activate the hippocampus into a higher state of alertness.

Stressing about a test can actually be beneficial as long as it isn't debilitating. Moderate amounts of stress activate the hippocampus, leading to more alertness and better memory.

The hippocampus forms what is called explicit, or declarative, memory. This kind of memory includes things that you have read or heard, events that have occurred, and people you have met. It also is involved in the formation of spatial memory, which allows you to find your way from one place to another. The hippocampus is large in animals such as squirrels that have to remember where they have stored food for the winter. London cab drivers must pass an exam that requires an exhaustive knowledge of the London streets. Researchers found that the hippocampus in these cab drivers was larger than average.

Whereas moderate, short-term stress helps you remember, severe stress can impair your memory. For example, Cushing's syndrome is a disorder in which there is an excess of cortisol. It causes muscle wasting, weakness, hypertension (high blood pressure), diabetes, reduced resistance to infection, and mental problems. Experiments have demonstrated that high doses of synthetic corticoid hormones disrupt memory in healthy volunteers. Stress, with the resulting natural increase in cortisol levels, has the same detrimental effect on memory.

Studies have demonstrated that in patients with Cushing's syndrome, post-traumatic stress disorder, and major depression, the hippocampus is smaller. Evidence shows that long-term exposure to stress and to elevated levels of stress hormones can damage both the structure and the functioning of the hippocampus.

The amygdala, a structure near the hippocampus, is the brain's center for responding to danger or strong emotions. You probably can't remember exactly what you ate for dinner on March 23 of last year, but you probably do remember what you were doing on September 11, 2001, the day of the terrorist attacks in New York City and near Washington, D.C. You also tend to recall details about important happy events, such as winning an award or getting married. These memories become fixed because they have a strong emotional content. You don't have to make an effort to recall them as you would if you were trying to recall the subjunctive form of a French verb. These kinds of memories are formed with the help of the amygdala. It is a survival system that stimulates you to action without your having to think about it.

The amygdala and the hippocampus are connected to the cortex, the "thinking" part of the brain. Through these connections, you form associations and learn what to fear. A good example of this involves an experiment with rats. Scientists give rats mild shocks repeatedly and at the same time sound a tone. After a while, the rats show a fear response whenever they hear the tone, even though it is not accompanied by a shock.

Sleep Deprivation

Everyone has had the experience of wrestling with a problem without solving it, then going to bed and "sleeping on it." After a good night's sleep, you may wake up with the answer. Something must have been going on in your brain while you slept.

The brain goes through cycles of different kinds of sleep: shallow sleep, during which you are easily awakened; deep sleep; and rapid eye movement (REM) sleep, when you have dreams. Some areas of the brain are more active during REM sleep than during wakefulness.

Scientists know that sleep is important, but they don't know exactly why. Some scientists think it is needed to restore energy. Others think that sleep helps the brain get rid of some memories while reinforcing others.

Many people find it hard to fit everything into their busy schedule. If you are a teenager, you probably sacrifice some sleep to squeeze all your activities into your day. Another problem for adolescents is that at late puberty, there is a change in the biological rhythms that control when people sleep and stay awake, known as the sleep-wake cycle. Teenagers may not be sleepy until two in the morning, and they can't get the amount of sleep they need if they have to get to school early in the morning. Adolescents need more sleep than younger children and adults, about nine hours a night, but many get only seven hours or fewer and are constantly sleep deprived.

Not getting enough sleep is stressful. During normal sleep, the levels of stress hormones decline. If you are deprived of sleep, the levels rise and the activity of the sympathetic nervous system increases. Experiments have shown that animals deprived of sleep die sooner. Both animals and people show especially marked stress reactions if they are deprived of REM sleep.

Lack of sleep affects your ability to learn. It can impair your abstract thinking, creativity, mental sharpness, decision making, and problem solving. In addition, if you are sleep deprived, it's more difficult to retrieve information from long-term memory. Sleep deprivation can make you moody and irritable and can impair your immune system, making you more prone to illness. Experts speculate that many automobile accidents involving teenagers may be related to sleep deprivation.

Lack of sleep can activate the stress response, but the opposite can happen as well. Stress in your life can disrupt your sleep. About 75 percent of people with insomnia have some serious stress in their lives.

Teen Brains

Even with a good night's sleep, being a teenager is stressful. The teenage years bring many new feelings and experiences. You are getting in touch with your feelings, testing your own strengths and abilities, and making plans for the future. Parents often complain that adolescents are moody, confused, rebellious, and reckless. Drug addiction, binge drinking, mental disorders, accidental deaths, and homicides are more likely to show up during this time of life. Until recently, most adults blamed raging hormones for teenage turmoil. Hormones do play a part, along with genetic, social, and environmental factors but so do changes in your brain.

Because the brain attains about 95 percent of its growth by the age of six years, scientists thought that it did not change much after that. But recent research has shown that many structural changes are still occurring in the brain during adolescence. Your brain isn't fully mature until at least eighteen years of age and probably isn't finished maturing until you are twenty-five.

Connections between nerve cells increase before puberty. Then, during adolescence, these circuits are reshaped. The reshaping happens mainly in the prefrontal cortex, the area of the brain that is involved in learning, planning, organizing information, and problem solving. Unused connections are pruned, and heavily used connections are strengthened. The connections between the prefrontal cortex and the emotional centers of the brain are among the last to be fully formed.

Dr. Jay Giedd, a child psychiatrist and neuroscientist at the National Institute of Mental Health, has done extensive research using brain imaging techniques. He believes that "use it or lose it" is a good motto to heed during adolescence and that it matters greatly what teens do during this period when the brain is still being shaped. Do you want to become a good soccer player, learn to play an instrument, or study a foreign language? This is the time to do it. Those connections in your brain will be hardwired.

Unfortunately, many teens experiment with dangerous substances, especially if they are under stress. Evidence shows that if you begin using alcohol, drugs, or nicotine during your adolescent years, you are more likely to become addicted than if you start as an adult. Teenage brains and adult brains respond differently to drugs. Adolescent rats and humans learn faster than adults, whether it's a maze or an addiction. Nicotine use during the teenage years can actually change your brain. It can cause the brain's wiring to develop inappropriately, according to Duke University Medical Center researcher Dr. Edward Levin.

What you do as an adolescent can have effects that last through adulthood. While your brain is still forming, many things can go wrong. Severe stress in early life—such as emotional, physical, or sexual abuse; violence toward the mother; and living with household members who were substance abusers, mentally ill, suicidal, or criminals—has far-reaching consequences in later life. These include a higher risk of depression, suicide, post-traumatic stress disorder, problems with learning and memory, substance abuse, and disorders such as heart disease, obesity, and cancer. You can learn more about some of these consequences in the following chapters.

Chapter 4

Stress and Your Heart, Immune System, and Gut

"If you leave me, you will break my heart." These words are not usually taken literally, but many doctors have been reporting cases of sudden emotional stress causing heart failure. Broken heart syndrome can be caused by grief, fear, anger, or shock, and it is the kind of heart problem from which victims recover when properly treated. These are not cases of sudden death like those mentioned previously but cases where stress hormones temporarily impair normal heart function.

The patients do not have blood clots, diseased arteries, or patches of dead heart muscle. They have a weakening of the heart that temporarily decreases its ability to pump. For example, a sixty-year-old woman suffered from broken heart syndrome, which doctors call stress cardiomyopathy, after seventy people jumped out at her from the dark and screamed "Happy Birthday!" She did not have a heart problem before her birthday and did not have one after being treated.

Doctors believe that the surge of adrenaline and other stress hormones stun the heart muscle during broken heart syndrome. They found that those who suffer from it are almost all female. These women had unusually high levels of stress-related chemicals and hormones at the time of the episode. In fact, they have been found to have seven to thirty-four times the normal level of adrenaline and related stress hormones. This rise in hormone level may temporarily impair heart functions, although doctors are not certain how this works, and some are skeptical that the syndrome even exists.

The triggers of broken heart syndrome, such as psychological stress, overexcitement, fear, and anger, do not usually cause permanent damage, but they may—especially if the person has heart disease. In that case, they may even cause sudden death.

Stress and the Cardiovascular System

The cardiovascular system refers to the heart and the many miles of blood vessels in your body. Chronic stress can lead to damaged blood vessels and heart attack (coronary infarction), in which the heart muscle is permanently damaged. Added risks are smoking, poor diet, obesity, high blood pressure, and inactivity.

Adam was a typical case in which stress led to unhealthful behavior. He was under stress most of the time. Adam's parents demanded that he make the honor roll at school, and he wanted to please them. But Adam was much more interested in his guitar and composing music than in anything academic. His hours on weekends were irregular, especially when he played with a band. And rehearsals took up more time than homework. Every time he practiced at home, his parents gave him grief about his grades. Why couldn't they understand that he was going to be a musician, and his courses at school weren't important to his future?

Adam relieved his stress by eating potato chips and ice cream. When his parents weren't home for dinner, he grabbed a hamburger and fries at the fast-food restaurant around the corner. He always felt rushed because he put off doing things until the last minute. He couldn't find time to exercise. His eating habits were causing his waistline to expand, and his stressed-out state was raising his blood pressure.

Adam didn't realize it, but his chronically elevated blood pressure was causing small areas of damage and inflammation in the smooth lining of his arteries. When this happens, fatty deposits and other circulating materials accumulate at the damaged areas, forming hard plaques. Plaque can obstruct the flow of blood in the artery, or it can break off and be carried to a smaller artery, where it can block the vessel, cutting off the blood supply completely. If plaque blocks the flow of blood to an area in the brain, it causes a stroke. If it blocks the flow of blood to a coronary artery (blood vessel that supplies the heart muscle), it causes chest pain or a heart attack. A heart attack occurs when the

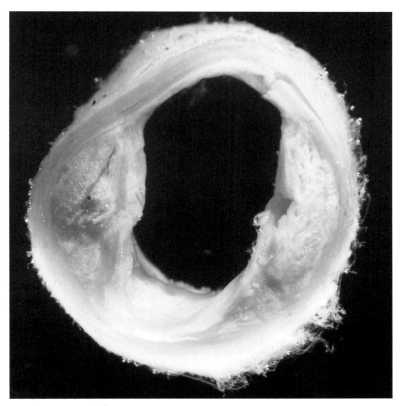

This is a section of an aorta, the main artery leaving the heart,
that has plaque on the left and the right of the aortic cavity.

blood supply is cut off completely and the muscle dies.

Heart attacks are uncommon in young people, but research has shown that damage to the cardiovascular system can begin in childhood or adolescence. Doctors are concerned about the growing numbers of children and teenagers whose unhealthful way of life places them at risk. Stress hormones increase appetite and increase the storage of fat, especially around the abdomen. This creates an apple-shaped body, with a waist that is bigger than the hips. In contrast, if most of the fat is around the hips and buttocks, the body shape is more like a pear. People who are apple shaped are more at risk for cardiovascular disease and diabetes than those who are pear shaped. With his stressful life, high-fat diet, apple-shaped obesity, high blood pressure, and lack of exercise—in addition to a family history of heart disease—Adam was headed for a heart attack or diabetes at an early age.

Doctors have recognized stress as a risk factor for heart attacks and stroke for many years. The risk for coronary heart disease is three to five times greater in people with higher levels of anger and anxiety compared with people who have lower levels. People with excessive competitive drive, aggressiveness, impatience, and a sense of time urgency along with hostility and insecurity are considered cardiac prone. Many of them do not realize they are overstressed. They don't realize that anything is wrong with their lives until a heart attack slows them down. Even moderate levels of worry have been associated with heart problems. One study, cited in the article "Stress and Heart Problems," found that people with mild worries were at almost twice the risk of heart problems.

Having some control over one's activities lessens the risk of heart problems. Dr. Eric Brunner, a senior lecturer at University College London, has said, "There is no doubt that people who occupy jobs which are repetitive, where they have little control over what they are doing, do have a higher risk of heart disease." Stress management is often part of the treatment for heart disease.

Your Immune System and Stress

Every time Nassim had to turn in a paper for English class, he was under a great deal of stress. He would always put the assignment off until a few days before it was due. Then he had to rush to the library and hope the books he needed were still on reserve. Nassim struggled with English, since it was a second language for him. And he needed to get a passing grade in English so he would not flunk out of school. Every time Nassim wrote a paper, he got a cold.

The colds were not surprising. A direct connection exists between stress and the immune system. The autonomic nervous system sends nerve branches to immune system tissue. Stress hormones also act on the immune system. If you are chronically stressed, the part of the brain that controls the stress response will be constantly pumping out a lot of stress hormones. The immune cells are being bathed in molecules that are telling them to stop fighting. So your immune cells are less able to respond to invaders such as bacteria or viruses. People with chronic stress show a prolonged healing time, a decreased ability of their immune systems to respond to vaccination, and an increased susceptibility to viral infections such as the common cold.

Autoimmune diseases—for example, rheumatoid arthritis—are conditions in which your immune system doesn't recognize your body's own cells and attacks them as though they were foreign intruders. Several factors are involved in autoimmune diseases, but at least part of the problem seems to involve the brain's hormonal stress response, according to Dr. Esther Sternberg of the National Institute of Mental Health.

Normally, cortisol keeps the immune system under control. But in many people with autoimmune disease, the body does not produce enough of this hormone to keep the immune system from attacking the body's tissues. This results in inflammation and damage to tissues and organs.

Stress, Premature Aging, and the Immune System

A recent study has shown that prolonged stress can actually make you age faster. It hastens the aging of body cells. Chromosomes are in the nuclei (control center) of your cells. They carry your hereditary traits. Telomeres are special structures that support the chromosomes. Telomeres are controlled by a substance known as telomerase. The activity of telomerase declines as you age. Each time a cell divides, the chromosomes lose a bit of material and the chance of the cell surviving is lowered.

Scientists studied women who were under prolonged stress because they were caring for a chronically ill child. They found that women who had been caring for their ill children the longest had the shortest telomeres and the least active telomerase. High levels of stress hormones raise the amount of oxygen free radicals—harmful chemicals that can combine with any tissue in the body and produce damage by reducing the activity of telomerase. This process may accelerate the aging of immune system cells by shortening their telomeres. The researchers believe that in this way chronic stress may weaken the immune system.

Stress and Your Digestive System

You have probably seen many stressed-out people gulping antacids on television shows. You may have experienced problems with your own digestion when you were under stress. For instance, your mouth gets dry because you have stopped secreting saliva. You may not know how the rest of your digestive system is affected, but the whole system feels your stress.

Stress hormones lower the release of stomach acid and other chemicals needed for digestion. Your small intestines stop absorbing nourishment and contracting their muscular walls, an action that normally squeezes digested food downstream. You don't need food in your fight-or-flight mode, because when you have to run from a specific threat, you don't want to be weighted down by the waste matter in your large intestines. When you are really frightened, diarrhea may occur (though why this happens is still unclear). In long periods of stress, constipation may occur.

Consider a condition known as irritable bowel syndrome (IBS). IBS is a very common gastrointestinal (GI) disorder, and one of the most common disorders triggered by stress. A person who suffers from IBS might experience abdominal pain, bloating, gas, and passage of mucus. Some people have diarrhea, while others have constipation.

Diarrhea is the result of increased contractions of the colon. It is commonly caused by bacteria or viruses or diseases such as colitis or cancer. But these are not the causes in IBS. Constipation results when the contractions become disorganized, so that there is little movement of intestinal contents toward the anus. People with IBS have GI tracts that are super-sensitive to stress. For example, some people might always be bothered by constipation when on vacation away from home but not at home when following their usual routine.

Gastric Ulcers

Although not as common as diarrhea and constipation, ulcers of the digestive system are also associated with stress. An ulcer is an inflamed area on the skin or in the lining of the wall of an organ. A gastric ulcer is an ulcer in the lining of the stomach. At one time, doctors thought that all stomach ulcers were caused by stress. But modern doctors know that a bacterium named *Helicobacter pylori* can live in the acidic atmosphere of the stomach and contribute to ulcer formation. It is present in about 85 percent of the people who suffer from gastric ulcers, and fortunately, the bacterium can be killed by antibiotics. But the bacterium is not the whole story. Many people who are infected with the bacterium don't get ulcers.

People who get ulcers may have a genetic tendency to secrete a lot of acid. Some of them may not make enough mucus in their stomachs to protect their stomach linings from the acid. Studies also show that the people who get ulcers are likely to be those who are stressed. Stress causes some people to smoke and drink, and this also may make them more vulnerable to gastric ulcers.

Perhaps you are wondering why stress should be involved in ulcer formation when stress cuts down on the amount of acid that is released into the stomach. Scientists explain that when there is less acid, the amount of mucus that protects the lining of the stomach decreases. Stress increases the rate at which ulcers are formed and decreases the rate at which they heal.

Chapter 5

Stress and Mental Disorders

Bill had a stepfather who was an alcoholic with a violent temper. He regularly abused Bill's mother and once even fired a gun at her. Bill witnessed this terrible event, but the next day, seemingly unaffected, he went off to kindergarten as though nothing out of the ordinary had happened. This child grew up to become the forty-second president of the United States.

Although Bill Clinton's childhood was chaotic, he survived the stress of living in a dysfunctional family. Countless others like him have also survived traumatic childhoods and adversity without any lasting emotional problems and have become successful and happy adults.

Who Are Resilient, and Who Are Vulnerable?

Child development experts have been puzzled that some people don't show emotional scars even after years of childhood neglect and stress. These people have a quality known as resilience—the ability to experience stress and bounce back.

People who deal well with stress have some traits in common: a positive attitude, a good self-image, good intellectual functioning, control over their impulses, ability to talk about their feelings, a capacity for dealing with problems actively, and unselfish concern for others. In addition, a social network of supportive family, friends, or mentors is very important. Despite growing up in poverty with mentally ill, abusive, or neglectful parents, people who possess the positive and supportive traits seem to be more resilient to stress.

Other children are born with personality traits that may predispose them to the risk of psychological disorders. About 20 percent of children have an inherited predisposition to overreact—an exaggerated fight-or-flight reaction, even in situations that others might not find at all stressful. Some are very cautious and shy in unfamiliar situations.

Genetics

In addition to environment and personality traits, genes and brain chemistry may also play a role in the way people respond to stressful childhood experiences. Genes are chemical units that determine hereditary traits passed from one generation to the next. Scientists studied a particular gene involved in the production of a substance known as MAO-A.

MAO-A is a chemical that breaks down other body chemicals called neurotransmitters. (Neurotransmitters are substances released by nerve cells. Neurotransmitters are involved in the transmission of messages between cells in the nervous system.) Low levels of MAO-A have been linked to aggressive behavior in mice and humans.

Researchers studied a group of seven-year-old boys in Great Britain. They found that child abuse and low levels of MAO-A both independently increased the risk of all types of mental health problems—not just aggressive behavior. Children with high levels of MAO-A had a lowered risk of mental health problems from child abuse.

Scientists have also found that a neurotransmitter known as neuropeptide Y seems to protect people against the effects of stress. They studied people undergoing military training in the U.S. Army and Navy. Those who had high levels of neuropeptide Y performed better in highly stressful situations than those who had lower levels of the substance.

Researchers still need to learn more about how genes, environment, and stress play a part in the development of mental illness. But they do know that anxiety disorders and depression are conditions that may be triggered by stress.

Anxiety

Anxiety is a sense of apprehension, dread, foreboding, or a worry that something awful is going to happen.

Suppose it's the end of the school year and you are about to take your math final. Tests are stressful, and you are a bit anxious. This is good stress. Getting revved up will help you do well on the exam. Your stress in this case is a healthy response, and it's normal. On the other hand, too much anxiety can be the main symptom of a group of conditions called anxiety disorders. Anxiety disorders are associated with over-active stress responses that don't get turned off.

Fear is a reaction to a real threat, mobilizing the fight-or-flight response. In contrast, anxiety is a state that feels like fear, but either the stress can't be identified or the worry is inappropriate or unreasonable. Thoughts and ideas alone can activate the amygdala and provoke anxiety even when no outside source of stress exists. Anxiety may range from vague feelings of uneasiness to bouts of terror. When you are anxious, your body may react with the same physical symptoms that are part of the fight-or-flight response, such as dry mouth, sweating, racing heartbeat, and tense muscles.

Anxiety disorders are among the most common mental disorders in all age groups. More than 40 million adults in the United States are affected. Thirteen out of one hundred children and adolescents between the ages of nine and seventeen suffer from some type of anxiety. About half of them have a second anxiety disorder or some other condition such as depression or behavioral problems. Anxiety can also be a symptom in many mental disorders, such as schizophrenia and dementia. Drug abuse and some medical conditions can cause anxiety too.

Anxiety may occur in various forms, such as generalized anxiety disorder (GAD), separation anxiety, phobias, panic disorder, obsessive-compulsive disorder (OCD), and post-traumatic stress disorder. Except for PTSD, often no obvious cause or stress triggers some of these conditions. As noted, genes, an overactive amygdala, overactive stress circuit response, temperament, and environment all play a part in a person's risk for developing an anxiety disorder or other mental illness.

Generalized Anxiety Disorder

Sixteen-year-old Gina had always been a good student and conscientious about her work, but lately, she felt irritable and restless and was having trouble concentrating. She couldn't seem to stop worrying about almost everything—her schoolwork, her father's health, and her performance during the last soccer match. She wasn't sleeping well, and when she went to bed, she worried that she might not be able to fall asleep.

Although she was an honor student, she fretted about the chances of getting into college. She couldn't shake the feeling that something terrible might happen, although there was no real reason to think so. Her condition went beyond everyday normal teenage worry. Her worries were excessive and interfered with her life. Gina was suffering from generalized anxiety disorder.

An estimated 5 percent of the population has had GAD during their lives, and about two-thirds of them are women. Over half of the adults being treated for GAD report that their symptoms started when they were children. About one-third also experienced depression at some time.

Phobias

While GAD involves free-floating, or general, anxiety about everything, phobias are irrational fears that are focused on specific things or situations that trigger intense anxiety. Some common phobias are fear of heights, fear of specific animals, fear of injections or blood, fear of enclosed places such as elevators or tunnels, and social phobia. Agoraphobia is the fear of leaving home.

Some phobias may be triggered by a memory of a frightening incident in the past or may be the result of a learned response. For instance, if a ferocious dog attacked you in the past, you might have a phobia about dogs. Or perhaps your mother was overprotective when you were a small child, and she warned you repeatedly not to go near any dogs. Often, however, it is not possible to identify the cause of these intense, unreasonable fears.

People with phobias aren't delusional. They realize that their fears are excessive and unreasonable, but they avoid the things or situations that trigger their anxiety. Suppose you have a phobia about snakes, and even going near the reptile house at the zoo makes you very anxious and uncomfortable. You might miss seeing some interesting creatures if you avoid the reptile house, but it wouldn't affect your life very much.

Other phobias can severely limit a person's normal daily life, social activities, and work or school performance. People with social phobia fear doing something embarrassing in front of other people. The most common social phobia is a fear of public speaking. Social phobia can be especially devastating for young people. Erin felt fearful in almost every social situation. She would get sick to her stomach, her heart would pound, and her palms got sweaty even before arriving at school or before a party or other gathering.

When she was with people, she felt embarrassed, she blushed, couldn't think of anything to say, and felt as though everyone was looking at her and judging her. Even though she knew these feelings were irrational, she couldn't control them. She couldn't go on dates, and sometimes she couldn't make herself go to school. Erin's family made sure she received appropriate treatment (discussed at the end of this chapter). Within three months, she had stopped experiencing overwhelming anxiety attacks in school or at social gatherings.

Obsessive-Compulsive Disorder

Obsessive-compulsive disorder (OCD) involves repetitive thoughts and behavior that are very hard to stop even though they are unwanted and distressing. Obsessions are persistent and intrusive thoughts that cause anxiety. The most common are fear of contamination by germs or dirt, repeated doubts, need for things to be in a certain order, and violent or sexual thoughts that are repugnant or against your beliefs.

Compulsions are repetitive rituals that are carried out to prevent or reduce the anxiety that accompanies the obsession. People with this disorder don't derive pleasure from their rituals but carry them out to get relief from the anxiety that occurs if they don't perform them. If you are obsessed by fear of germs, you might spend hours every day washing your hands until they are raw. If the routine is disturbed, you would become anxious and feel compelled to start over again.

Sean was obsessed with counting everything. He had to count all the lines in whatever he was reading, and he counted the fence posts on his street every day on his way to work. He became very anxious and felt that something bad might happen if he didn't perform these rituals. Sean knew that his disturbing thoughts and rituals were completely irrational. They took up so much time that he wasn't able to do the things he wanted to do, but he couldn't stop them until he got therapy.

Scientists are trying to discover what goes on in the brains of people who suffer from OCD. They think a problem exists with the circuit that connects the frontal lobes of the cortex with another part of the brain called the basal ganglia. The frontal lobes preside over decision making, judgment, and planning. The basal ganglia filter messages to and from the cortex. A procedure called functional brain imaging has provided evidence suggesting that parts of the basal ganglia and cortex are overactive and do not work normally in people with OCD.

One known cause of obsessive-compulsive symptoms is injury or disease that affects the basal ganglia. Some researchers have suggested that another cause might be a type of common bacterial infection—the kind that causes strep throat. When bacteria invade, your immune system produces antibodies to attack the infection. But sometimes things go wrong, and these antibodies attack the body's own tissues. The researchers theorize that in children, the antibodies may attack the basal ganglia in the brain, causing symptoms of OCD.

Separation Anxiety

About one in every twenty-five children has difficulty leaving his or her parents to go to school or camp or to spend the night at a friend's house. They are clingy and fearful and may worry that they will be kidnapped or that their parents might die. Some are even afraid to go to birthday parties.

Six-year-old Greg had always been clingy and shy, anxious in new situations, and wary of strangers. He would get upset and cry whenever his mother left him with the babysitter. When he started kindergarten, Greg had a difficult time. He delayed leaving for school in the morning, crying and clinging to his mother. On school days, he often complained about having a stomachache or headache, but not on weekends.

Young children normally start to show some fear about being separated from their parents at about one year old. This fear peaks at about the age of two. It usually slowly diminishes. By about the age of six or seven, it typically disappears. If it persists in older children and becomes a problem, it is called separation anxiety disorder.

It usually shows up when children start school, as in Greg's case. Sometimes it happens later, when children move from elementary school to middle school. Other triggers may be a move to a different neighborhood or changes within the family, such as a new baby or a divorce. Another contributing factor in the child's environment may be parents who are overprotective, abusive, or inconsistent or who fail to provide sufficient support and encouragement to their children.

Studies of adoptions and twins show that heredity plays a part in separation anxiety disorder. Children who are shy, clingy, fearful of strangers, and anxious in unfamiliar situations seem to be more prone to develop separation anxiety and other anxiety disorders.

Post-Traumatic Stress Disorder

Fifteen-year-old Erica's house burned down after her brother was playing with matches in the room next to her bedroom. Everyone in the family escaped without injury, but they were all frightened and sad as they watched the flames destroy their house. The firefighters would not let Erica go back in the house to collect her favorite things even after the fire was out.

Erica's family had to move to her grandmother's house while theirs was being repaired. Erica felt irritable and angry all the time, and she was easily startled. She blamed herself for not watching her brother more carefully and worried about his starting another fire. Her mother noticed that she seemed withdrawn and wasn't interested in activities she used to enjoy.

Erica had trouble eating and sleeping even three months after the fire. She had nightmares from which she awakened in a cold sweat and a state of fright. The nightmares were not always about the fire, but they were very real and scary. Every so often, she would get a flashback—a sudden, vivid memory of the fire, usually triggered by something that reminded her of the event. When her father lit a fire in the fireplace, the sight and smell of the burning logs made her feel as though the house fire were happening all over again. She became frightened and panicky.

Erica tried to avoid thinking about the fire, and she tried to suppress her feelings about the event.

She didn't want to be reminded of the fire, so she didn't go back to her house while she was still living at her grandmother's. Erica did everything she could to stop the memories. When Erica's nightmares and feelings of anger wouldn't go away, her mother took her to the doctor to talk about what was happening. They learned that Erica was suffering from post-traumatic stress disorder (PTSD).

After a disaster, victims experience a range of emotional response. Certain symptoms of PTSD are an appropriate response to a terrifying event. A very large majority of people—over 90 percent—who have had traumatic experiences do not develop PTSD. Some report that they have grown stronger after the experience. Most people recover over the first three to six months, but if the symptoms last longer than three months, they are considered part of a disorder. Symptoms usually begin within three months of the event, but sometimes they are delayed as long as years after the traumatic experience.

Psychiatrists define a traumatic event as an experience that "involves a threat (or reality) of death, serious injury, or damage to physical integrity, and inspires intense fear, helplessness, or horror." Some events that may cause PTSD are rape or other sexual abuse; physical abuse; violent crimes or kidnappings; and natural disasters such as hurricanes, tornadoes, or earthquakes; and airplane or car crashes. Being in a war or witnessing death and destruction or other terrible and scary experiences can also cause PTSD. But events that distress one person may not affect another in the same way.

Sometimes PTSD is caused by events that don't

62

involve threats to physical safety. Illness, divorce, or job loss can lead to PTSD. According to a survey of university students, about half the events they experienced did not fall under the definition of trauma. But the people who had PTSD symptoms suffered just as much anxiety and pain as those who had experienced severe trauma.

After the initial experience, a PTSD sufferer reexperiences the upsetting event in a number of ways. The person may have recurrent and distressing memories of the event, frequent dreams about it, or intense anxiety when confronted with anything that triggers memories of the event. The person may also experience flashbacks. Someone who is having a flashback may lose touch with reality and believe that the traumatic event is actually happening again. He or she avoids thinking or talking about the event and avoids places, people, or things that are reminders.

Diminished interest in normal activities, a sense of detachment, and a feeling of numbness occurs. In addition, the person may have difficulty sleeping and concentrating, may be irritable, startle easily, or have outbursts of anger. About one-third of people who develop PTSD have chronic symptoms that do not go away. They may have personality changes, moodiness, self-destructive behavior, shame, hopelessness, or difficulty in relating to other people.

Hector and his friend were walking down the street when his friend was suddenly gunned down in a drive-by shooting. He did not talk about the experience to his classmates or teachers, but his participation in school activities declined as did his grades. He was afraid to ride his bicycle near the park where his friend was shot. From time to time, he had visions of the shooting, and he felt irritable and depressed. The counselor at Hector's school directed him to a group therapy program to share his experience and participate in mental exercises that helped him reduce his anxiety. His grades improved, and he seemed more relaxed and "living in the present."

The risk of developing PTSD seems to depend more on the characteristics of the individual than on

Many people who experienced Hurricane Katrina in 2005 and the surrounding events developed post-traumatic stress disorder. These two sisters lost their home in Bay Saint Louis, Mississippi, during the hurricane. They had to camp on their lawn for many days afterward.

the nature of the experience. Women are more at risk than men. People who have had previous traumatic experiences are at greater risk. Depression, anxiety disorders, other psychological disorders, and alcohol or drug abuse are other factors that increase vulnerability to PTSD.

Treatment for Anxiety Disorders

Everyone experiences unavoidable stress in life, but there are ways of managing it. Chapters 7 and 8 discuss some of these strategies. But sometimes self-help methods aren't enough. If the anxiety is overwhelming and it interferes with a person's life, treatment from a mental health professional may be needed.

People with anxiety disorders can be helped in a variety of ways, including psychotherapy, drugs, and relaxation techniques to control muscle tension. Psychotherapy is a treatment for psychological disorders based on verbal communication between the therapist and patient. Many different types exist, but the object of all psychotherapy is to help people recognize their problems so that they can make positive changes. The most effective kind of psychotherapy for some anxiety disorders seems to be cognitive behavioral therapy, or CBT.

Cognitive behavioral therapy helps you change the way you think so that you have more control over your feelings and reactions. You learn new and better ways to deal with these anxious feelings. CBT is based on the premise that your thoughts influence how you feel and what you do. It helps people to recognize faulty patterns of thinking and to replace them with more positive thoughts.

Another helpful treatment is behavioral therapy, which involves exposure to the anxiety-provoking situation or object. The person is gradually exposed to the feared situation, with the aim of eventually eliminating the anxiety. This technique is especially helpful in treating phobias.

Take the case of Hector, whose friend was shot and killed. Hector's therapist encouraged him to recall the incident in detail and describe it to the others in his group. It was very difficult for him at first, but he gradually became less anxious. Reexperiencing the incident in a safe place and receiving emotional support helped Hector defuse the anxiety associated with the bad memories. Eventually he was even able to return to the park where the shooting took place without feeling a surge of terror. His mood improved, and he felt like his old self again. When he thinks about the shooting, he feels sad, but he is no longer troubled by frightening flashbacks.

Stress and Depression

Everyone feels sad, blue, or down in the dumps sometimes. But the disorder that psychiatrists call clinical depression isn't just about feeling blue. It's a state of mind that doesn't go away in a short period of time, and it interferes with the way people think, feel, and behave.

Depression, like anxiety disorders, can be the result of abuse and neglect in childhood. Stresses in early life, heredity, and temperament all have an influence.

Depressive disorders affect an estimated 6 to 10 percent of adults and as many as one of every twenty children and adolescents in the United States.

Depression has been called the common cold of mental health because it affects so many people.

Symptoms Of Depression

How do you know whether a depression is serious? You may be suffering from more than just a temporary blue mood if you have experienced some of the following symptoms for at least two weeks:

- sad or tearful mood or, instead (especially children and teenagers), irritable or angry or show rebellious or aggressive behavior
- loss of interest or pleasure in activities that were once enjoyable
- loss of appetite or overeating
- insomnia or sleeping too much
- feeling slowed down and tired all the time or restless
- feeling bored all the time
- difficulty in focusing, thinking, or remembering
- feeling hopeless and helpless
- feeling worthless and guilty
- thoughts of suicide

Signs of depression are sometimes not recognized when the illness masquerades as physical problems such as fatigue, weight loss, headaches, or stomachaches. Symptoms may vary in different cultures.

Causes

Depression is not just one disease, and its causes are multiple. It can result from some medical conditions. Certain medications and illegal drugs can cause

67

A group of teens meets to talk about their problems in an after-school support group. Support groups and group therapy sessions can help with depression and anxiety disorders.

symptoms of depression as well. Major life events such as the loss of a loved one, getting divorced, moving, or retiring can trigger depression. Even positive events such as winning an important award may cause depression. Natural disasters, physical and emotional abuse, family conflicts, and social isolation are other stressful events that can trigger both depression and anxiety.

Many times, no direct cause can be found. In addition to the influence of heredity and recent stress, the most common predictor of major depression in adults is a history of abuse in childhood.

Depression seems to run in families. An individual who has close relatives with a history of severe depression is more likely to develop depression than someone in the general population. If one of two siblings in a family has a history of depression, there is a 25 percent chance that the other will suffer from depression.

Identical twins share all their genes. If they live in the same household and one has depression, the other has a 76 percent chance of developing the illness. If they are raised apart and one twin develops depression, the other has a 67 percent chance of becoming depressed. This is a much higher risk than in the general population.

Researchers have identified a gene that increases the risk of depression. If you have one version of the gene, it doesn't mean that you are destined to become seriously depressed. It means that you may be more vulnerable to stresses in the environment. Probably multiple genes interact with one another to contribute to depression.

As noted earlier, people who have been exposed to prolonged stress show changes in their brains, such as a decrease in the size of the hippocampus. The hippocampus is also smaller in individuals with a history of depression. The more prolonged the depression, the smaller the hippocampus. Depression is similar to a stress response that hasn't been turned off, with elevated levels of the stress hormone cortisol and abnormal levels of the chemical messengers serotonin, dopamine, and noradrenaline.

Stress and Learned Helplessness

When animals are subjected to stress, they show reactions that resemble human depression. For

69

example, researchers have done experiments in which a previously unstressed rat is placed in an area divided into two halves. At intervals the rat receives a mild shock in one half or the other, preceded by a signal that tells it which side is going to be electrified. The rat quickly learns to move away from the half about to be electrified when it hears the signal.

The results are very different when the experiment is done with a rat that has been recently exposed to repeated stresses from which it could not escape. The stressed rat cannot learn to move away from the half about to be electrified when it hears the signal. It has learned that it is helpless to control its environment.

Depression can be caused by and lead to social isolation.
Symptoms of depression include sadness and
loss of interest in everyday activities.

Dr. Martin E. P. Seligman and other researchers believe that the behavior of rats with learned helplessness parallels some of the symptoms seen in humans with severe depression. The rats can't cope with life. They seem to give up trying. Similarly, severely depressed people may stop showing interest in their day-to-day activities. They may neglect their personal hygiene, lose interest in food and sex, and show sleep disturbances.

Severe stress in real life may be a factor in producing the learned helplessness of depression in some people who are more vulnerable. Not everyone who is subjected to severe trauma reacts with depression or anxiety disorders, but if the stress is severe enough, anyone is vulnerable.

Treatment for Depression

Treatment for depression involves medication and psychotherapy. Just as CBT effectively treats anxiety disorders, it also treats depression in people with distorted beliefs and learned helplessness. Many effective antidepressant drugs work by altering the levels of various brain chemicals. Many drugs for depression increase the amount of serotonin in the brain.

Chapter 6

Are You in Control?

No two people experience stress exactly the same way. But one huge difference in how they handle stressful situations is whether they are in control of the situation or believe they are in control. Scientists have known the importance of control for many years. As far back as the mid-1960s, Drs. Martin E. P. Seligman and Steven Maier at the University of Pennsylvania did research with rats that showed the importance of being in control.

They injected some rats with tumor-causing cancer cells. All the rats were also given electrical shocks. Some of the rats could escape from the shocks by moving to another part of the cage while others couldn't escape from the shocks. Those who could escape from the shocks were less likely to get cancer. Those who could not escape from the shocks had no control over their stress and therefore were more likely to get cancer.

Just the thought of being in control can help a person experience less stress. Have you ever been to the dentist when he asks you to lift your finger if he causes you a great deal of pain? He implies that he will stop, but he probably could not. Most people do not find the need to raise a finger, partly because they think they have some control of the painful experience.

One illustration of the importance of the feeling of control is that of a pilot flying an airplane next to an aircraft carrier. The wings of the plane are at right angles to the deck of the carrier. The occupants of the plane are highly stressed, except for the pilot, who knows he is in control and can bring the plane to a position where it will land safely on the deck.

Sometimes the fight-or-flight reaction can occur during periods of calm. The memory of fearful events may prime your body to overreact to everyday situations. Your body may react to stresses even before they happen. Suppose you have to go to a clinic to have blood drawn for a test. You hate having a hypodermic needle stuck in your arm. As the technician prepares it, your arm starts to throb even though she has not touched your skin.

You cannot always be in control of a stressful situation. Perhaps you believe that you can achieve what you want by working harder and by staying with a problem until you get the results you want. You believe that something insurmountable can be accomplished if you handle the situation in the right way. Or you believe that stress can be avoided if you do the "right thing." However, at times you have no control over a stressful situation. You have control only over how you cope with the situation.

Terrorism

Terrorism has made fear and caution a bigger part of everyone's life than ever before. Since the terrorist attacks on the World Trade Center and the Pentagon on September 11, 2001, stress about bombings, biological warfare, chemical attacks, and nuclear exposure has increased. No one knows what might happen next. People tend to overreact right after a terrorist disaster and underreact when the memory fades.

Preparing for emergency action can reduce stress levels. Many people prepare for potential emergencies by readying small bags containing their medicines and a battery-powered radio. This gives them some feeling of control over the general feeling of unease that exists because of terrorism.

Many teens have discussed emergency measures with their parents and carry identification cards with them. Many keep cell phones with them on which they have emergency numbers. Learning first aid from the Red Cross can also be a good way to deal with stress over terrorism and stress of almost any kind. Stress levels decrease when you feel prepared.

Hurricanes, Tornadoes, and Other Weather Stressors

Hurricanes, tornadoes, and other severe weather can cause a great deal of stress for many people. On

August 29, 2005, Hurricane Katrina destroyed the city of New Orleans, Louisiana. The city had been built below sea level and was guarded by 350 miles of levees (embankments to prevent flooding). Levees did not hold the storm surge, and a twenty-five-foot wall of water flooded the city.

The water destroyed about 160,000 homes in New Orleans. Many thousands of people had to evacuate. Rescue workers lifted residents into helicopters from the rooftops where they had fled the rising water. Some parts of the city were not as badly damaged, but the city suffered more than at any time in its history.

The cities of Gulfport and Biloxi, Mississippi, and many rural areas on the Gulf Coast also suffered severe damage from Hurricane Katrina. Thousands of victims there and in New Orleans suffered days and months of almost unbelievable stress. Imagine having no food or water for days while worrying about the safety of family and friends and the destruction of your home. More than one in ten evacuees reported that a family member, a neighbor, or a friend had died in the storm. All Americans who watched television, read about the disaster, and who worked to help the victims experienced the stress of Hurricane Katrina to some degree.

You may never experience the stress of a hurricane that floods your house or endangers your life. But people who live where floods, tornadoes, earthquakes, windstorms, dust storms, or other natural disasters have occurred may suffer an unconscious amount of stress about the possibility of severe weather damage happening again. Although people have no control over severe weather, they can be somewhat in control

A helicopter rescues these residents from the floodwaters of Hurricane Katrina on September 1, 2005. Severe weather such as hurricanes effects large numbers of people at the same time.

by planning for it. Many people worry less about severe weather when they keep emergency kits with a flashlight, battery radio, and other emergency items in case they lose power. Many residents who live on the shore reduce their stress about floods by storing material for boarding up windows.

Loss of a Loved One

Losing a parent, a close friend, or a pet causes people to experience the stress of grief. Grief is the reaction to loss. The grief process includes denial, anger, guilt, and sadness. These are normal reactions, but they do not always happen in the order that many books on grief suggest. Denial, numbness, and disbelief are normal at first, and feelings of pain, fear, and helplessness are common. These feelings help people tolerate the loss until they gradually accept it.

Although people have no control over the loss of a loved one, they can decrease the stress by mourning. This can include crying, talking about the person who died, and sharing memories. People who are allowed to mourn openly usually move through their grief faster than those who try to be strong and "just get over it." Grief becomes less intense over time, but it may not ever fade completely.

Bullying

Bullies look for attention by picking on kids their same age or younger for no apparent reason. Bullies hurt people physically, call them names, grab their belongings, exclude them from a group, threaten them, and do all sorts of things to make themselves feel important. Usually they don't care about the feelings of others.

Robert Cormier, a famous young adult author, wrote about a bully who attacked him on his way to and from school. He tells how he tried to avoid the bully by taking different routes. This worked for him, but often victims cannot avoid bullies because they are on the playground with them, in the same locker rooms, or eat in the same school cafeteria. They may find help if they report the bully to a teacher, but many victims of bullies are too embarrassed to ask for help.

Children who are bullied suffer physically and mentally. Some victims of bullying have been known

Being bullied sometimes comes in the form of being excluded from a group.

to commit suicide. For example, one boy hanged himself after suffering repeated abuse by a bully. He left a suicide note describing a particularly painful incident in which the bully had stolen money his grandmother had given him for a haircut. He ended up cutting his hair himself. The boy's diary revealed many other abuses he'd suffered at the hands of his bully.

Many schools have programs that help teachers and students take action against bullies. No one deserves or needs to put up with the stress of being bullied. If this happens to you, stay with others, and get help from an adult.

Dating Violence

Recent statistics indicate that you or someone you know will probably experience the stress of dating violence. Estimates of dating violence among middle school and high school students range from 28 percent to 96 percent. This includes physical abuse, such as hitting, slapping, or hurting with a knife or other weapon, as well as emotional, sexual, and psychological abuse. In addition to name calling, emotional abuse includes extreme jealousy, possessiveness, and efforts to control your time with friends or family.

Hannah had been in a close relationship with Barry for almost a year. He was handsome, brilliant, and everything Hannah had ever wanted. But he was very possessive of her. He didn't like her to spend time with other people. The couple often went to concerts alone. When they were driving home from one of the best concerts ever, Barry insisted they should make it a memorable night by having sex. Hannah said she was not ready. When he insisted, he threatened to break up their relationship.

Barry said if he could not have her, no one else would. Without her, life was not worth living. He threatened to drive the car into the lake. Hannah jumped out of the car and ran toward a house. The people who lived there helped her. Before they drove her home, they called the National Domestic Violence Hotline at (800) 799-SAFE. The hotline worker told Hannah about a group in her community who could help her with her problem.

If you (or your friend) are in a dating relationship that in any way makes you feel uncomfortable, awkward, tense, or frightened, trust your feelings and get out of it. It could become or may already be abusive. Remember, you have the right to say no. No boyfriend or girlfriend has the right to tell you what you can or should do, what you can or should wear, or what kind of friends you should have. Don't let a boyfriend or girlfriend be a source of stress to you. Call the hotline, or talk to an adult that you trust.

Road Rage

Jared pulled his car into the left lane near the traffic light. He was unaware that the driver of the car behind him was planning a left turn. The light turned red and Jared stopped. The driver who pulled up on his right side was furious. He gave him the finger, lowered his window, and screamed at Jared.

This caused Jared considerable stress, but he knew he could defuse the situation by staying calm. He gave an apologetic wave and then turned his eyes to the road in front of him. He did not react with anger. He knew that an angry response would only escalate the situation.

Smoking and Drinking

Smoking can reduce stress in the short run. It improves mood, relaxes muscles, and increases problem solving in the short term. The first cigarette is usually unpleasant, but after the first few, smoking a cigarette is often a calming experience. One reason is that the stress of the body's craving for nicotine is relieved. People can become addicted to the nicotine in tobacco after smoking just a few cigarettes, and that addiction is hard to break.

You see many ads for products that claim to help people stop smoking. Although not everyone who smokes cigarettes becomes addicted to the nicotine, many people do. You can't tell ahead of time whether you are one who will become addicted and suffer the stress of craving a cigarette and of trying to quit smoking. Quitting is extremely stressful, and many who try do not succeed without trying several times. Some smokers are never able to quit.

Pressure on young people to try smoking has declined somewhat, since there is less social acceptance of smoking and since more people know the health risks. The higher cost of cigarettes and fewer places to smoke them have helped reduce the stress that smokers put on nonsmokers. More states and cities are banning smoking in public places.

Drinking alcohol is another common tool used to cope with stress. After the first drink or two, most people feel relaxed. But the calm feelings do not last. Further drinking can make the drinker more vulnerable to stress than ever. Many people "who drown their sorrows in drink" suffer from depression after the effect of the alcohol has worn off. Some people become aggressive and even violent. Smoking cigarettes and overuse of alcohol are stressors, not ways to control stress.

Children of Alcoholics

One in five adult Americans lived with an alcoholic while growing up. Many children try to keep the alcoholism of a parent a secret. They do not bring friends home or explain why their clothes are not always clean, why they are sometimes late for school, or why they frequently have headaches and other illnesses that are brought on by too much stress.

Cara's father left his family because of her mother's drinking problem. Cara was left with the responsibility of taking care of her mother when she was drunk. Cara prepares all their meals. Day after day, she worries about losing her mother to an accident or illness caused by frequent drinking. Will she accidentally burn the house down when she is drunk? Will she fall and break her arm or her leg while Cara is at school? Cara hides her mother's problem from others. She is afraid to talk to the counselor at school for fear she will be put in a foster home.

Cara's mother has disappointed her so many times that she learned not to trust people. Cara feels lonely and helpless to change the situation. The stress of her mother's alcoholism affects the chance of Cara having a healthy and happy childhood and will affect her life as an adult because of the emotions she learned as a child.

Britlyn has a different problem with alcoholism. Her mother is very supportive, but her father drinks too much. He is usually a pleasant, peaceful man, but when he has had too much to drink, he becomes violent. Sometimes he abuses Britlyn's mother, but her mother will not report the abuse to the police. Her mother says he didn't mean to hurt her, and when her father promises he won't do it again, she believes him.

Britlyn's father has sexually abused her, but she knows that if she told her mother she would not believe her. If Britlyn would confide in her teacher, a counselor at school, or a family member she trusts, she might no longer have to suffer the abuse and stress of a drunken father.

Both Cara and Britlyn feel that their lives are out of control. Both might be able to reduce their level of stress and bring their lives under control by asking for help.

Some Other Stressors

Certain stressors cannot be controlled. Discrimination due to race, handicap, gender, sexual orientation, and age are on the long list of stresses you cannot control. Lack of control over your physical environment can cause considerable emotional, mental, and physical stress. For example, violence in school and in neighborhoods causes stress to a great many people. For those stressors that can't be changed, learning to manage the stress is especially important.

Chapter 7

Outwitting Stress through Meditation

Tessa came home from her first year at boarding school to find that her stepmother had completely refurnished the house. All the rooms had lost the wonderful, familiar look her mother had given them. Tessa's mother had died a year ago, and Tessa found comfort in the familiar surroundings when she came home for the holidays. She could never feel at home again. She hated her stepmother even more than she had before. The stress of living in this family was ruining her life.

A friend suggested that Tessa practice the serenity prayer to help her reduce the stress. "God grant me the serenity to accept the things I cannot change, courage to change the things I can, and wisdom to know the difference." This is the prayer that helps those who attend Alcoholics Anonymous and many other support groups. It helps many people who are stressed out, even people who aren't religious but can understand and appreciate the prayer's message. It helped Tessa accept that her stepmother was in charge of the house and things would never be the same as when her mother was alive.

Many stresses come from sources that can't be changed. For example, fourteen-year-old Brian had to live with the stress of a broken marriage. His mother and father still fought over where he would spend holidays and how often his father could take him on weekend vacations. He had to accept being shuttled back and forth between parents. Brian could not control the stressful situation he was in, but he learned to accept the problem by realizing it was something he could not change.

Farah's stress

Farah thought she could outwit her stress. Whenever Farah became upset by the stress of being called fat, she ate more. She knew this made things worse, but she ate to cover the feelings of self-hatred.

Eating eased the emotional pain, but the stigma of living in the fat lane caused more stress. Farah felt hungry all day, so she nibbled on candy and cookies. She kept telling herself she would start another crash diet next week, so the extra food wouldn't matter. She did diet every few weeks, and she usually lost about three pounds each time. But when she was dieting, she felt miserable, deprived, and irritable, so

Stress causes many people to overeat. In some cases, people will binge eat when they are extremely stressed. This means they eat an excessive amount of food in a short period of time.

she soon gave up the diet, and the weight came right back again.

Farah was a fast eater. She gobbled down her food without tasting it because she needed to comfort herself. Her sister, Angela, was thin and beautiful. This made matters worse, especially when Angela got a job as a model. Farah was so stressed out she decided to give up trying to get thin. She hid food in her room so she would always have something to eat when she was hungry. Her friends nagged her about her weight, but the food made her feel better temporarily, so she chose it over her friends.

Help came when Farah's doctor told her to join a stress management class that was meeting in her community once a week for six weeks. She learned to handle her stress by living one day at a time. She planned her food for the day each morning. She tried to remember that if she worked at the program just this moment, she could do it. She learned a relaxation technique called body scanning, which included tensing and relaxing her muscle groups.

Body Scanning

You can reduce stress by tensing and relaxing muscles in different parts of your body and focusing on sensations as you go. Make a fist with one hand, and feel the tension in your fingers and the palm of your hand. Relax your hand, and notice the difference in feeling. A body scan helps you to learn which parts of your body are tense and need relaxing.

Tense each muscle group for about six to seven seconds, relax the muscles, and then repeat the tension and relaxing. Breathe out as you relax muscle groups.

Feet: Feet tend to cramp when muscles are tightened, so tense these muscles only slightly for three seconds. Begin by turning your feet slightly downward, turning them slightly inward, and curling your toes.

Calves: Point your toes upward and then downward.

Thighs and buttocks: While sitting, lift your legs straight out in front of you. Or tense your buttocks and thighs by squeezing the muscles.

Stomach: Pull your stomach in, and hold it there so that it feels hard.

Shoulders and upper back: Pull your shoulders up as if strings were attached to them from the ceiling.

Chest: Take a deep breath, and hold it for about six seconds. When you breathe out, do so easily and gently.

Hands: Make a fist. Note any tension in your wrist. After you relax your hand, tense individual fingers.

Face: Frown and knit your brows. After you relax your forehead, squint your eyes and wrinkle your nose. Next, clench your teeth, and pull back the corners of your mouth. Press your tongue against the roof of your mouth. Then with teeth separated, press your lips together.

Practice tensing and relaxing each muscle group several times a day. You may find you enjoy doing this. If a muscle group remains tense, practice relaxing it more often.

In another form of body scanning, you can move your breath slowly through various parts of your body. Begin at the feet, and end at the head, where you can pretend to breathe out through a hole in the top of your head. Body scanning can be used alone or before the relaxation response.

The Relaxation Response

The relaxation response is based on meditations of Buddhist monks and other ancient practices. It is opposite to the fight-or-flight reaction, for it quiets the mind and decreases blood pressure, breathing rate, and metabolism. Dr. Herbert Benson, a Harvard physician, described the relaxation response about a quarter of a century ago. It became a popular way to reduce stress and help heal many illnesses.

You can learn the relaxation response at home, sitting in a quiet place, and breathing slowly and deeply while you cast out all other thoughts. Can you do this for five to ten minutes? It sounds easy, but it really is very difficult, and it takes a lot of practice and patience. You might begin with a variation known as the quieting reflex.

Learning To Relax with the Quieting Reflex

Many kinds of relaxation response techniques exist. The quieting reflex is a mini-relaxation technique that helps as soon as a stressful situation arises. It can be done any place and takes only a few minutes.

Step One: Decide what is causing your stress.

Step Two: Say to yourself, "Alert mind. Calm body." Repeat this several times.

Step Three: Smile to yourself. This relaxes your facial muscles.

Step Four: Inhale slowly, imagining that your breath begins at the bottom of your feet. Feel your breath move upward through your body. Count one to three. Exhale slowly and pretend the breath is gradually returning to your feet.

Repeat this quieting reflex several times a day. It is best to sit in a chair in a quiet place, but it may help no matter where you are.

Try the Real Thing

To learn to meditate, you will need to find a quiet place. Use earplugs if you cannot find a quiet spot.

The temperature should be comfortable and the lighting soft. Lie down with your feet or legs elevated, or sit in a comfortable chair, without crossing your legs. Decide whether you want to use a mantra, a word that you will repeat with each breath. Some people use "ah" as a mantra, and others count.

Tell yourself you are going to breathe deeply without thinking about anything else. Or focus on one thing, such as a babbling stream, a lake, or the ocean. You are going to train your mind to think of one thing for a period of time. Close your eyes, and take a deep breath. Slowly breathe out, and take another deep breath. If you are using a mantra, silently say the word each time you breathe in and when you breathe out.

If your mind wanders, bring it back to a still place. Don't be discouraged if you cannot think of just the mantra or one thing for a long time. Learning to meditate takes patience. You may wish to start with a five-minute period and gradually increase it to thirty. Some people find it best to set aside the same period of time for meditation each day.

Belly breathing helps reduce stress too. If you place your hand on your abdomen while you are meditating, you will notice that you can feel your belly expand when you breathe in. Perhaps you have been told at some time to "pull in your gut." Actually, when people panic, they tend to breathe from the chest instead of the belly. Breathing rapidly from the chest increases stress, but belly breathing during meditation helps reduce stress and sensations of panic.

When you regularly meditate, your mind will become clear and still, free of negative and wasteful thoughts when you finish each day. You will experience a new sense of peace, self-awareness, and self-acceptance. Meditation has been compared to letting clouds or mist dissolve to reveal a clear sky with a shining sun. After you practice meditation for a while, you will probably notice that you can handle a crisis with more ease.

Kinds of Meditation

While the relaxation response is used in lots of mind-body techniques, there are many variations of it. But two steps are present in all of them. One is the repetition of a word, thought, sound, prayer, image, or muscular action. The other is a passive attitude toward intruding thoughts.

Meditation is not dependent on any belief system, but it is a part of the great traditions, the enduring systems of belief, such as Christianity, Judaism, Buddhism, Shinto, Islam, and Hinduism. Buddhism is the tradition most closely associated with meditation.

Buddhism meditation: While Buddhism is a religion to about 300 to 350 million people around the world, it is also a philosophy of life. Buddha is not considered a god but a man who taught a path to enlightenment through love and wisdom. At the age of thirty-five, Buddha attained the state of Nirvana, the enlightened mind, after sitting under a tree in solitary meditation for forty-nine days. Buddha taught his followers that meditation is essential to the spiritual life. Statues of Buddha are commonly seen in a posture of meditation. One of the Buddhist teachings is that wealth does not bring happiness. Buddhism teaches that the solutions to our problems are within ourselves, not outside.

Concentrative meditation: This technique directs the mind to a single focus such as a mantra or breathing. You might concentrate on an image, an icon, or a relaxing scene such as a body of water or a mountain vista when you meditate. Concentrating by watching a flame or the flames in a fireplace works well for some people. All meditation relies on concentrating, but concentrative meditation emphasizes a certain thing.

Guided imagery: This form of meditation uses visualization of a soothing scene that is pleasurable to you. Place yourself at the scene, and call on your senses to fill in the picture. If you are in the kitchen when freshly baked apple pie is ready to come out of the oven, you are sitting at the table sensing the wonderful odor. Your mouth is watering. The warmth from the oven spreads over your back. You think about the wonderful taste of apple pie. You can call up this pleasant scene time and again. Or you could picture yourself on a sandy beach enjoying the breeze and the heat of the sun. You might see yourself in a field of wildflowers. You can use any memory that pleases you. Take deep breaths for five or ten minutes while picturing the pleasing image.

Loving-kindness meditation: The mantra used for loving-kindness meditation is "May I be well" or "May I be at peace." After a short time of saying one of these mantras, the person who is meditating changes the "I" in the mantra to the name of a friend. Including other people in the meditation helps to develop a healthy relationship with others. After a period of meditation, the mantra is changed to include a person who is not a close acquaintance. Then the meditation wishing this neutral person well is changed to include the name of someone who has been the source of conflict. The last stage in this kind of meditation uses the mantra, "May we be well," or "May we be in harmony."

Mindfulness meditation: Mindfulness is a way of looking deeply into oneself in the spirit of self-inquiry and self-understanding. Although it is similar to Buddhist meditation, it is not based on any belief system. *Mindfulness* means "paying attention on purpose in a particular way in the present moment." It is the opposite of taking life for granted.

Living in the moment is a theme that runs through many methods of coping with stress. Some programs open with the leader of a group distributing three raisins to each person. Everyone is asked to look carefully at one raisin and to notice its color, shape, odor, and size. They study the raisin for several minutes and try to keep other thoughts from intruding. Then the one raisin is eaten with awareness, noting the movement of the arm and hand as it is brought to the lips. Salivating is noticed, and the raisin's taste and texture and even the chewing experience are all part of the awareness of eating the raisin. Then the group proceeds to examine the second raisin. And then the group examines the third. At this point, the participants have already begun to reduce their anxiety.

The Stress Reduction Clinic at the University of Massachusetts Medical Center is famous for teaching mindful meditation. It is described in two books by Dr. Jon Kabat-Zinn: *Wherever You Go, There You Are: Mindfulness Meditation in Everyday Life* and *Full Catastrophe Living*.

Religious meditation: This kind of meditation has been used for thousands of years, and it is still used by Christians, Jews, Muslims, and others. It is focused thinking that, like other kinds of meditation, takes serious effort. It is a refocusing from the world and reflecting on God's or Allah's word. (The Bible mentions "meditate" or "meditation" twenty times.) Long and focused prayers are considered a kind of meditation. Prayer, in fact, is the most commonly used form.

Sufi dancing or walking: This kind of meditation was developed in medieval Islam, but it can be used by people of any faith. It is walking or dancing in groups that seek mystical unity and ecstasy. Chanting of sacred phrases, moving in rhythm, and breathing in harmony help participants feel connected with all life.

Tai chi: This meditation involves deep breathing and a series of postures during which you inhale and exhale slowly. Slow, graceful movements increase strength and flexibility and improve balance and circulation. Certain movements that are combined with undivided attention help heal and revitalize both body and mind.

Tai chi originated in China as part of Taoist religious practices, but it is no longer used only in religion. It is practiced in twenty-five countries worldwide, and there are many varieties. Taoist tai chi specifically deals with health problems.

Walking meditation: With this kind of meditation, you walk slowly while focusing on your legs and feet. You think of each movement: lifting, moving, and placing. The first step is to notice the feeling of your feet touching the floor. Your arms should hang naturally, and hands should be clasped in front. Focus your eyes on the ground about two feet in front of you. Concentrate on the sole of your foot. Try to concentrate on the walking experience, and when your mind wanders, bring it back to the lifting and dropping of walking.

Yoga: Various forms of yoga popular in the United States are simplified versions of the yoga of Hinduism.

Yoga can be practiced alone or in a group. This group of students is practicing a cross-legged pose.

They teach different bodily postures that increase self-awareness and relieve stress. The popular cross-legged position (the lotus pose) that is a famous meditation posture has been used for at least five thousand years.

Yoga teaches disciplined behavior, control of breathing, positive values, meditation, and more. Hatha yoga stresses bodily postures and breathing techniques with emphasis on better health. Some other forms of yoga emphasize understanding of the soul. Serious yogis practice to achieve their goal of isolation of the soul from the body and mind.

Meditation and the Body

Reducing stress is among the many benefits of meditation. According to some studies, meditation can lower blood pressure, reduce pain, and lower the production of stress hormones. The pain of arthritis, cancer, AIDS, and other diseases has been reduced by people who meditate. Even the pain of migraine headaches can be lessened through meditation. In some experiments, meditation has been a factor in increasing the number of antibodies after flu shots and in faster recovery from other illness.

Some people think meditation works only because people believe it works, but scientific studies suggest that meditation may be able to change the brain. Intensive and regular meditation may alter the way the brain is wired. Some neuroscientists say that much more experimentation must be carried out before they will accept that meditation can train the brain to generate compassion and positive thoughts. Regardless, people who practice meditation appear to

be able to deal with stress better than those who don't.

Dr. Herbert Benson tells some amazing tales of Tibetan monks in India. They experience very low rates of oxygen consumption during meditation. But this is not quite as surprising as something else they are able to do: drying wet sheets on their bodies in wintry conditions!

Picture twelve monks sitting in a chilly room waiting until three in the morning when the temperature has reached forty degrees. At a signal from their leader, the monks take off their clothes with the exception of small loin cloths. They sit cross-legged on the floor and dip sheets, measuring about three by six feet, into pails of water. The water is about forty-nine degrees. They pick up the sheets, wring out most of the water, and wrap them around their upper bodies.

The monks start to meditate. The sheets cling to their bodies, but the monks do not shiver. The monks sit there calmly, and in about three to five minutes, the sheets begin to steam. Within about forty minutes, the sheets are completely dry. The monks repeat this procedure twice before leaving the room.

This procedure has been documented by filmmakers from the Western world. The monks can raise their skin temperatures by meditating. Somehow, the monks in their meditation are able to generate heat from the fat in their bodies. Scientists once thought that only animals that hibernate could do this. How the monks can stand the cold without shivering and actually dry wet sheets on their bodies is still a mystery. But it certainly shows that control of the mind can affect the body.

You may want to try different kinds of meditation. The kind you choose is not as important as how often you practice it. Try to practice once or twice a day. Choose a time, such as before breakfast, and stick to it each day. Routine will help to enhance a sense of ritual. Don't be discouraged if you miss a day. Meditation feels good. It can help you manage stress and take control of your life.

Chapter 8

More Tools for Reducing Stress

A fictional community of people lived along the banks of a river. Over time, a large number of men, women, and children fell into the river and had to be rescued from drowning. The community posted lifeguards along the river banks, bought ambulance speedboats, and everyone learned how to revive drowning people. One day someone asked, "Why don't these people learn to swim?" Sometimes, an answer is so obvious that it is overlooked.

New stresses will become part of your life as long as you live, but many don't know how to cope with them. There are numerous simple ways to deal with stress. Some ways take self-discipline, but they are free and can be learned without cost or pain. The more control you have over stress, the better your life will be.

Control "What-If" Thinking

You have an interview about a summer job. It's a job at the beach, putting up umbrellas, renting beach chairs, and cleaning the beach each morning. It pays good money, and half the time, you can sit on the beach and read a book.

As the day for the interview nears, you start to wonder about your chances. Will your references be good enough? Maybe someone will tell the interviewer about the job you blew at the drugstore. That was a year ago, but word does get around. What if the boss thinks you don't look old enough? Maybe he won't like your hair. There are lots of things to worry about, and you find all of them. The more you worry, the more you feel stressed out. To stop what-if thinking, you can substitute thinking about a plan that you will follow in case this interview doesn't go well. What is the worst-case scenario? Are there other jobs that might be just as good?

People who tend to obsess over what can go wrong suffer unneeded stress. Most worry is founded more on things that don't happen than on those that do, and worry is a stress in its own right.

Justin was worried about having to be at his grandmother's house when the long-distance movers brought her furniture. She was away for the summer, and no one was home at her house or even a neighbor's house. Suppose he got sick and couldn't be there. The movers would not be able to get in the house.

What would they do with the furniture? What if he had an accident or a flat tire when he was driving to his grandmother's house? How would he reach the movers?

Justin's stress was unnecessary. The night before the movers were to arrive, they called to give Justin their cell phone number. He could reach them in case of emergency. The next morning, he was at his grandmother's house an hour before the movers were supposed to arrive. When they called to say they couldn't find the way, Justin met them in town and showed them the way.

Do you have a tendency to stress yourself about things that might happen? Try to control the worry by reminding yourself that it will not change the outcome of the situation.

Stop Thinking Stressful Thoughts

Sometimes a stressful situation is remembered day after day. Ali's sister committed suicide by jumping from the roof of their high-rise apartment building. She had been suffering with severe depression ever since Ali could remember. Ali could not stop thinking about her every night, even many months after it happened. Again and again, she pictured her sister falling from the eighteen-story building. She could not let go of this stressful thought.

A therapist suggested that Ali use a mental stop sign whenever she started to think about her sister's suicide. She replaced the thought by saying "Stop!" to herself every time she started to think of her sister's tragic death. Instead, she thought about her brother playing soccer. This was always a happy picture. It took several weeks for Ali to control her stressful thoughts about her sister's suicide. But she gradually learned to think about it only occasionally and not to dwell on it.

Many stresses are exaggerated feelings, such as: "I'm always the one to get the seat in the back." "If I could be better, I wouldn't have to worry." "I lose everything." When you are feeling stressed over something, consider how important that something really is. Instead of looking at the weeds, can you see the flowers?

What you think about can trigger stress. Remember that most of the troubles you worry about will never happen. One way of controlling stressful, exaggerated feelings is to ask yourself how important the worrisome issue will be in five years.

Learning to Say No

Latisha was the only one in her family who could use a computer. Her brother, Jared, leaned on her whenever he needed a term paper typed. Latisha was glad to help him, but her time was getting scarce. She found herself typing for Jared's debating club when she wanted to have some free time of her own. Still, she didn't want to feel that she had let her brother down. Then a friend of her mother asked Latisha to find some recipes on the Internet and make copies for her. Each time she did some work for someone else, Latisha grew more stressed. She was getting further behind in her own work.

Latisha complained to her best friend, Emily, about the problem she was having. She wanted to help everyone. She hated to say no, but the extra work made her feel angry at the unfairness of the situation.

Emily asked Latisha if her world would fall apart if she explained her time problem to those who wanted her help. She could nicely say no to them. Latisha decided to explain to her brother and her mother that she was behind in her own schedule, and although she would like to help them, she had to say no. Saying no stressed Latisha somewhat, but it reduced her stress in the long term.

Many people agree to requests because they want other people to like them. Saying no to matters that can cause a problem is one way to avoid stress.

Having a Support System

Not having close friends can be as detrimental to your health as smoking or carrying extra weight. Many studies have shown that social ties reduce the risk of disease by lowering blood pressure, heart rate, and cholesterol. Community has been called one of the most basic of human needs.

Suppose you discover that you have a serious disease. This can be extremely stressful. Your stress can be lessened by family and friends and also by a support group of people who suffer from the same disease. The same can be true for other stressful situations. Almost everyone has heard of Alcoholics Anonymous, but there are many other support groups. Broken Spirits Network, for example, aids current victims and survivors of child abuse, sexual abuse, rape, and domestic violence. Gamblers Anonymous offers help for problem gamblers. And numerous support groups exist to help people quit smoking. Many of these groups have web-sites for more information.

The Power of Appreciation

You can develop a sense of appreciation by noting the good things in life. Focus on things that are beautiful, times when you experienced kindness, and when you had love in your heart. Petting a dog or thinking of a beautiful sunset can help relieve stress. Learn to see the good things in life and concentrate on them. Keep your thoughts away from negativity as much as possible.

Ryson hated school. He didn't have time to do his homework, and he was always in trouble with his teachers. He worked after school, and on weekends he was too stressed to have any fun. From the time he got up on Saturday morning until the time he went to bed on Sunday, he thought about how awful his life was. Nothing was any fun when you had to work every day after school. His grades were getting lower, and he worried that he would not be able to get into college.

Ryson's favorite teacher talked to him about the stress of working so much. He promised to help Ryson apply for grant money so he could cut back on his hours at work. Ryson's attitude changed. He enjoyed his weekends more, and he used them to have fun, meet new people, and do some of the schoolwork he had neglected when he was too depressed to tackle it.

Even though he still had to spend some time work-ing after school, he stopped looking at the bad side of his life. He learned to appreciate the kindness of his teacher and to see the good things around him as well as the bad. He noticed the beauty of the sky, the trees

that grew around him, the taste of the food he ate and, especially, the new friends he made.

Dealing with Peer Pressure

Peer pressure is when someone your age tries to get you to do something. It can be good or bad. Peers influence one another in good ways daily, from spreading the news of a good book to getting others to help with disabled classmates. Teens know when peer pressure is negative, such as when a kid influences another to shoplift, smoke, treat a classmate in a mean way, or do any number of things that they know are wrong.

Some teens go along with negative peer pressure because they want to be liked. They think others will make fun of them if they don't. They believe "everybody's doing it" when that may not be the case at all.

Teens who pay attention to their own feelings and beliefs walk away from peer pressure, even though it sometimes seems hard. Less stress occurs when two or more people stick together to avoid peer pressure. "I'm with you. Let's go," are good words for friends to use when they stick together to resist peer pressure. But even one person can overcome the stress of pressure to do something that is wrong by just walking away.

Less Stress in Taking Tests

Many teens consider academic pressure their biggest source of stress. Certainly, tests are a major stress for all teens in school. Some feel that they do best if they stay up studying all night before a test. But keeping a regular pattern of eating and sleeping is important to prevent you from feeling like a zombie on the day of the test.

Before you go to the test, be sure you have enough pencils and plenty of time so you don't feel rushed. Read the directions carefully, and survey the test to make sure you do not spend too much time on one part. If you get stuck on one question, go on to the next. If you have time at the end of the test, you can go back to it. Do the easy questions first. Guess if you don't know the answer, and remember that your first guess is usually the better one.

More Ways to Help Control Stress

Squeeze a stress ball. These soft balls come in a variety of sizes and colors.

Sleep eight or nine hours a night. Staying up much of the night and catching naps during the day does not fulfill your sleep needs. Sleep and stress are intricately woven. Sleep is both a response to stress and a prevention technique.

Pet a dog or cat.

Stay healthy by eating the right kinds of food, including fruits, vegetables, and whole grains. Avoid too much caffeine.

If you have a big task, break it into small parts.

Learn to feel good about doing something even though it is not done perfectly.

Turn to music. Listen to some of your favorite songs while you are cleaning up or doing something else that is stressful.

Take a break from something stressful by counting backward or imagining something pleasant such as

*Animals can help relieve stress. Dogs are used
for therapy in many hospitals, nursing homes,
and children's health centers* (above).

sailing on a lake with just the right kind of wind.

Dance around the room for a few minutes.

Exercise by stretching, taking a walk, running, or
doing a few yoga or tai chi movements.

Change your attitude. Much stress comes from
wishing a situation would be different. Dr. Jay Winner,
author of *Stress Management Made Simple: Effective Ways to
Beat Stress for Better Health*, says that "the present
moment can only be the way it is."

Keep a journal. Write things down to get them off your chest. You may wish to include ways to change a stressful situation.

Go outside for a few minutes of fresh air, no matter what the weather.

Sit or stand as if a string from above were pulling your head up. Bad posture can lead to muscle tension and increased stress.

Help someone. Get involved with a service project or volunteer to help a disabled neighbor. It is almost impossible to feel stressed out when helping someone else.

Don't procrastinate. Doing a difficult task right away instead of putting it off reduces stress.

These are just some of the things you can do to lessen stress. Perhaps you can add some of your own ideas to the list.

Glossary

acute stress: short-term stress

adrenal glands: paired glands above the kidneys. They secrete the hormones adrenaline (epinephrine), noradrenaline (nor-epinephrine), and cortisol, which are involved in the stress response.

adrenaline: hormone secreted by the adrenal glands

adrenocorticotropic hormone (ACTH): pituitary hormone that stimulates the adrenal glands to produce cortisol

allostasis: stability through change. Allostatic systems keep the body stable by changing in response to stressful challenges.

amygdala: structure in the brain involved in emotions such as anxiety and fear

antibodies: proteins released in the blood in response to certain substances that they attack and destroy

anxiety: excessive worry out of proportion to the situation or feelings of apprehension without an obvious cause; may range from feelings of uneasiness to terror and panic

arteries: blood vessels that carry blood from the heart

autoimmune disease: disease in which the immune system does not recognize the body's own cells as "self" and attacks them as foreign invaders. Examples are rheumatoid arthritis and multiple sclerosis.

autonomic nervous system: part of the nervous system that controls heartbeat, blood pressure, breathing, digestion, and other functions not under voluntary control. Its two components are the sympathetic and the parasympathetic nervous systems.

broken heart syndrome: a weakening of the heart that temporarily decreases its ability to pump

carbohydrates: one of the three main classes of food needed by the body

cardiomyopathy: disease of the heart muscle

chromosome: a tiny, threadlike substance in animal and plant cells that carry genes

chronic stress: frequent periods of stress; repeated stress that activates a person's stress response again and again

cognitive behavioral therapy (CBT): psychotherapy that involves identifying anxiety-provoking, negative thoughts and feelings; changing these patterns of thinking; and learning better ways of dealing with anxiety or depression

compulsions: rituals that are carried out to prevent or reduce the anxiety that accompanies an obsession

corticotropin-releasing hormone (CRH): hormone released by the hypothalamus, stimulating the pituitary gland to release adrenocorticotropic hormone (ACTH)

cortisol: stress hormone produced by the adrenals

Cushing's syndrome: disorder caused by certain tumors or excess secretion of ACTH by the pituitary gland, resulting in elevated levels of cortisol or related hormones; can cause hypertension, diabetes, mental problems, and other conditions

depression: symptoms lasting two weeks or more that may include sad or tearful mood; anger or hostility; loss of interest or pleasure in activities previously enjoyed; sleep problems; loss of appetite or overeating; feeling tired, bored, restless, helpless, and hopeless; and having thoughts of suicide

dopamine: chemical involved in transmission of messages in nervous system

endocrine glands: organs that release chemical substances called hormones into the bloodstream. Hormones travel to various parts or organs of the body and influence their functions. The pituitary, adrenals, thyroid, and pancreas are examples of endocrine glands.

endorphins: natural painkillers produced by the body

fatty acids: complex molecules derived from fats

fight-or-flight response: the body's response to perceived threat or danger

gastric ulcer: stomach ulcer; an inflamed area in the mucous membrane (lining) of the stomach

gene: a unit of heredity located in a specific place on a chromosome

glucose: simple sugar utilized by the body for energy. Carbohydrates are broken down to glucose in the body.

Helicobacter pylori: a bacterium that can cause gastric ulcers

hippocampus: structure in the brain involved in memory

hormone: chemical substance secreted by an endocrine gland and released into the bloodstream. A hormone acts on other organs or parts of the body. The body produces many hormones.

hypertension: high blood pressure

hypothalamic-pituitary-adrenal axis (HPA axis): also called the stress circuit; system that controls the activity of many hormones and allows the body to respond to challenges

hypothalamus: part of the brain involved with the functions of the autonomic nervous system and with the endocrine system; plays a role in the stress circuit

immune system: complex system that protects the body against infectious agents such as bacteria and viruses; recognizes the difference between body cells and outside invaders

irritable bowel syndrome (IBS): a digestive disorder with no known organic cause, such as infection

mantra: word or sound used in prayer or meditation

neurotransmitters: chemicals that carry messages between nerve cells

noradrenaline: a hormone secreted by the adrenal glands

nucleus: structure in a plant or animal cell containing genetic material

obsessions: persistent and unwanted thoughts that cause anxiety

ovarian: relating to ovary. The ovaries are female sex organs.

panic disorder: attack of terror accompanied by symptoms such as pounding heart, sweating, chest pain, nausea, fear of losing control, or fear of dying

parasympathetic nervous system: part of the autonomic nervous system responsible for calming the body; has effects opposite from those of the sympathetic nervous system

phobia: irrational fear focused on specific situations or things that trigger extreme anxiety. Some common examples are social gatherings, heights, enclosed places, snakes, and blood.

pituitary: endocrine gland in your head near the hypothalamus; called the master gland because it regulates and interacts with other endocrine glands in the body; part of the stress circuit (HPA axis)

plaque: a build up of fatty deposits, calcium, and cell debris in the lining of an artery

post-traumatic stress disorder (PTSD): disorder that may result after experiencing a traumatic event such as a natural disaster, an airplane crash, witnessing death or destruction, or being a victim of a violent crime

prefrontal cortex: area of the brain involved in learning, planning and organizing information, and problem solving

serotonin: chemical involved in transmission of messages in nervous system

sympathetic nervous system: part of the autonomic nervous system; set of nerves that help prepare the body for action; responsible for the fight-or-flight response

synapse: area through which impulses are transmitted between two nerve cells

telomeres: structures in the cell that cap the ends of chromosomes

ulcer: inflamed area on the skin or mucous membrane. A gastric ulcer is an inflamed area in the mucous membrane (lining) of the stomach.

voluntary nervous system: part of the nervous system under conscious control

Source Notes

46 Wendy Moore, "Stress and Heart Problems," *Channel4.com*, December 2002, http://www.channel4.com/health/microsites/0-9/4health/stress/aas_heart.html (October 4, 2007).

62 "Rethinking Posttraumatic Stress Disorder," *Harvard Mental Health Letter* 24, no. 2 (August 2007):2.

64 William R. Saltzman, "School Based Trauma and Grief Intervention for Adolescents," *Prevention Researcher* 10, no. 2 (April 2003):8–11.

107 Jay Winner, *Stress Management Made Simple: Effective Ways to Beat Stress for Better Health* (Santa Barbara, CA: Blue Fountain Press, 2003), 22.

Selected Bibliography

Allison, Kathleen Cahil. *Stress Control: A Special Health Report.* Boston: Harvard Health Publications, 2002.

Benson, Herbert. *Timeless Healing: The Power and Biology of Belief.* New York: Scribner, 1996.

Blair, Justice. *Who Gets Sick.* Houston: Peak Press, 1987.

Carlson, Richard. *Don't Sweat the Small Stuff and It's All Small Stuff.* New York: Hyperion, 1997.

Fox, Annie, and Ruth Kirshner. *Too Stressed to Think: A Teen Guide to Staying Sane When Life Makes You Crazy.* Minneapolis: Free Spirit Publishing, 2005.

Goleman, Daniel, and Joel Gurin, eds. *Mind Body Medicine: How to Use Your Mind for Better Health.* Yonkers, NY: Consumer Reports Books, 1993.

Hipp, Earl. *Fighting Invisible Tigers: A Stress Management Guide for Teens.* Minneapolis: Free Spirit Publishing, 1995.

Kabat-Zinn, Jon. *Full Catastrophe Living: Using the Wisdom of Your Body and Mind to Face Stress, Pain, and Illness.* New York: Delta Trade Paperbacks, 1990.

———. *Wherever You Go, There You Are: Mindfulness Meditation in Everyday Life.* New York: Hyperion, 2005.

Lenson, Barry. *Good Stress, Bad Stress*. New York: Marlowe and Company, 2002.

Luskin, Fred, and Kenneth R. Pelletier. *Stress Free for Good: 10 Scientifically Proven Life Skills for Health and Happiness*. New York: HarperCollins, 2005.

McEwen, Bruce S., and Elizabeth Norton Lasley. *The End of Stress As We Know It*. Washington, DC: Joseph Henry Press, 2004.

Moyers, Bill. *Healing and the Mind*. New York: Doubleday, 1993.

PBS. "Inside the Teen Brain." *Frontline*. Program 2011, first broadcast January 31, 2002, by PBS.

Restak, Richard. *The Mind*. New York: Bantam Books, 1988.

Rosenberg, Nancy. *Outwitting Stress: A Practical Guide to Conquering Stress Before You Crack*. Guilford, CT: Lyons Press, 2003.

Saltzman, William R. "School Based Trauma and Grief Intervention for Adolescents." *Prevention Researcher* 10, no. 2 (April 2003):8–11.

Sapolsky, Robert M. *Why Zebras Don't Get Ulcers: The Acclaimed Guide to Stress, Stress-Related Diseases, and Coping*. New York: Henry Holt, 2004.

Seaward, Brian Luke. *Stand Like Mountain, Flow Like Water*. Dearfield Beach, FL: Health Communications, 1997.

Talbott, Shawn. *The Cortisol Connection: Why Stress Makes You Fat and Ruins Your Health*. Alameda, CA: Hunter House, 2002.

Winner, Jay. *Stress Management Made Simple: Effective Ways to Beat Stress for Better Health*. Santa Barbara, CA: Blue Fountain Press, 2003.

For Further Information

Books

Canfield, Jack. *Chicken Soup for the Teenage Soul: The Real Deal Challenges: Stories about Disses, Losses, Messes, Stresses & More.* Deerfield Beach, FL: HCI Teens, 2006.

Ford, Emily, Michael Liebowitz, and Linda Wasmer Andrews. *What You Must Think of Me: A Firsthand Account of One Teenager's Experience with Social Anxiety Disorder.* New York: Oxford University Press, 2007.

Hyde, Margaret O., and Elizabeth Forsyth. *Depression: What You Need to Know.* Danbury, CT: Franklin Watts, 2002.

Hyde, Margaret O., and John F. Setaro. *Smoking 101: An Overview for Teens.* Minneapolis: Twenty-First Century Books, 2006.

Irwin, Cait, Dwight L. Evans, and Linda Wasmer Andrews. *Monochrome Days: A First-Hand Account of One Teenager's Experience with Depression.* New York: Oxford University Press, 2007.

Moragne, Wendy. *Depression.* Minneapolis: Twenty-First Century Books, 2001.

Pedrick, Cherry, and Bruce M. Hyman. *Anxiety Disorders.* Minneapolis: Twenty-First Century Books, 2006.

Seaward, Brian, and Linda Bartlett. *Hot Stones and Funny Bones: Teens Helping Teens Cope with Stress and Anger.* Deerfield Beach, FL: HCI Teens, 2002.

Wilde, Jerry. *More Hot Stuff to Help Kids Chill Out: The Anger and Stress Management Book.* Richmond, Indiana: LGR Publishing, 2001.

Websites

American Institute of Stress
    http://www.stress.org
    This website provides information on all stress-related subjects.

American Psychological Association
    http://helping.apa.org
    This association publishes articles on physical and psychological well-being.

Center for Mindfulness in Medicine, Health Care, and Society
    http://www.umassmed.edu/cfm/index.aspx
    This is the website for the mental health center at the University of Massachusetts Medical School.

Mental Health America
    http://www.nmha.org
    This is the official website for Mental Health America, formerly known as the National Mental Health Association, which focuses on the care and research of mental health.

National Institute of Mental Health
    http://www.nimh.nih.gov
    This is the official website for the U.S. government institutes of research on brain, mind, and behavior.

WebMD
    http://www.webmd.com
    This is a great website for accurate medical information.

Index

119